The
Miracle of Forgiveness

The Miracle of Forgiveness

A TRUE STORY

E. Miriam Murphy

The Miracle of Forgiveness
Published by E. Miriam Murphy
with Castle Publishing Ltd
New Zealand

© 2025 E. Miriam Murphy

ISBN 978-0-473-73922-5 (Softcover)
ISBN 978-0-473-73923-2 (ePUB)
ISBN 978-0-473-73924-9 (Kindle)

Editing:
Rachel Ross

Production & Typesetting:
Andrew Killick
Castle Publishing Services
www.castlepublishing.co.nz

Cover Design:
Paul Smith

All scripture quotations (unless otherwise stated)
are from The Holy Bible, English Standard Version®,
copyright © 2001 by Crossway Bibles,
a publishing ministry of Good News Publishers.
Used by permission. All rights reserved.
(See the back of this book for other versions used.)

ALL RIGHTS RESERVED

No part of this publication may be reproduced,
stored in a retrieval system, or transmitted
in any form or by any means, electronic, mechanical,
photocopying, recording or otherwise,
without prior written permission from the author.

*As Christians, we can't pretend there will never be dark days.
But as we face them, the dark times throw God's light
into sharp relief.
And can make us grateful for the smallest blessings
we are given every day.
And make us grateful to the One
who gives each day to us.
It is only through gratitude that we start to really
notice the true nature of our everlasting Father.*

Foreword

In late 2023, my precious sister shared much of this powerful story at my home church.

It took enormous courage to share details that, even after many years, were very raw – an incredibly difficult thing for her to do. It had a significant impact on those who heard it then, and I have no doubt it will have a significant impact on any who read it now.

A few days after she shared her story, I travelled with her to spend some time at her home. A 'debrief time', we called it, having no idea that, slowly but surely, Sis would open up about other stuff she hadn't previously shared.

The healing journey for any of us is so often like that. A process, not a sprint, best shared by those who love us, and know us. So often we expect instant healing of circumstances or sickness, and have our own ideas about what healing might look like. But I have learned that, frequently, healing cannot happen until we are prepared to be vulnerable, to be humble enough and brave enough to share our rawness – both with each other and with Jesus.

Before I returned home, I encouraged Sis to be obedient to God's call and write down what she had shared. Well she did, and I'm so proud of her courage and obedience. You are now holding her book in your hands.

Our stories need not be like this story to be powerful. Every time we share about God's goodness to us, we are planting seeds that the Holy Spirit can water. Perhaps when we share our stories something good grows – for us and those who hear it.

I know that Sis and I share the prayer that God's Holy Spirit will have His way for healing, for all who read this story. For His glory.

– Chris Beale

Contents

Acknowledgements	11
Part One: The Lesson of Forgiveness	**13**
1. Death Came Suddenly	15
2. Grief and Confusion	23
3. Jesus Came to Visit	33
4. The Lesson: Forgiveness	39
5. A Loving Ministry	51
6. Miracles	61
7. Mending Family Ties	71
8. A Final Hearing	75
9. Freedom at Last	81
10. It Takes a Lot of Love to Forgive	87
Part Two: The Hard Bits	**93**
11. The Cracks Start to Show	95
12. Betrayal	101
13. An Ending	107
14. He Never Left Me	115
Helpful Scriptures for Further Study	121
Author's Note	125
Notes	128

Acknowledgements

This testimony is dedicated to the Glory of God, who has shown me that His love is faithful, and His miracles are still available to us all every day. No matter what we go through, what we have done, or how great our sins are, He is still ready to forgive and bless a repentant heart. Thank you, Gentle Master.

And to my dear sister, Christine, who is also my sister in Christ. She has often been a great source of strength and encouragement, listening patiently as I told her this story in full, and gently encouraged me to write this book and to tell it all (even the hard bits). Thank you, Sis. Love you.

I need to acknowledge the help and support we received from the New Zealand Police. Their dedication and hard work, in very difficult circumstances, helped to bring the investigation and legal proceedings to a swift conclusion. My deep thanks go to the team that dealt with this case and to the detective in our local town who tried so hard to be of help without compromising the investigation. Thank you all.

Note: All names have been changed to protect the privacy of those involved.

PART ONE

The Lesson of Forgiveness

1

Death Came Suddenly

"What's for lunch, Mummy?" Five-year-old James strolled into the kitchen just as I had begun preparing sandwiches for him, his seven-year-old brother, Alex, their soon-to-be stepdad, Tom, and myself.

It was a wet, rainy Saturday, so we had planned to have a carpet picnic lunch in the living room and enjoy a TV movie together. But the phone rang just as the last of the food was being loaded onto a tray.

Wiping my hands clean, I reached for the phone. "Hello?"

After a long silence, "Hello, Miriam. It's Keith..." More silence. The tone of my brother-in-law's voice told me that something wasn't right.

"Keith, what's wrong? Are you OK?"

"It's Dad... Miriam... He has been found dead... They suspect he's been murdered."

"I'll get Tom to the phone," I stammered. "He will need to hear this from you."

I called out to Tom, letting him know his brother was on the phone with some bad news.

We had both lived through unhappy marriages and had decided to give love a second chance. Our wedding was planned for October 25th, 1986, and today's date was October 4th.

Picking up the tray, I took it to the boys in the living room, inviting them to eat. "We won't wait for Tom. He will be a while. Go ahead and help yourselves."

What little I could hear of the conversation from the hallway was very quiet. Tom listened intently as the full extent of what had happened was explained to him, and Keith answered what questions he could. Later, Tom confirmed that the police had advised that his father's car and firearm were missing, and his wallet had been emptied and left on the floor.

I didn't know it at the time, but there was a huge shift taking place during that phone call. It's not something I can truly explain even today, more than 35 years later. It was almost like the world gasped, and just for a second, all the air vanished from our home. (Even that doesn't completely cover the sense of terror I felt.)

After a short time, Tom returned to the living room, sat down and took a few bites of a sandwich. Nothing was said about the call, and I figured it would wait until later that evening when the children were in bed. But Tom had already begun to shut down.

In that moment, my life and the lives of my family were changed forever. Nothing was ever going to be quite the same again.

All the solid ground we thought our lives were built on was ripped away. But we could not possibly have known that God was about to lead us all (even the boys) on a nine-year odyssey through grief, pain, anger, acceptance, forgiveness and miracles. Things would happen during those nine years that the great Alfred Hitchcock himself could not have dreamed up. And the script... well, judge that for yourself. But it's all true. As God is my witness, it all happened.

My father-in-law, Willard, lived full-time in a caravan at a holiday park by the seaside, in the upper North Island of New Zealand. His brother Joe and his wife had a home just a few blocks away, and the two men spent a lot of time together. It was Joe who had called Keith with the news of Willard's death.

A week earlier, Joe and Willard had been out fishing together for most of the day. They had returned to Joe's house to clean their catch and have a bite to eat before Joe drove Willard back to his caravan home.

As the brothers usually spoke at least every other day, Joe had become concerned that he hadn't heard from Willard in a week. So, after visiting the site a couple of times during that week and not being able to reach his brother and not finding Willard's car parked in its usual place beside the caravan, Joe decided to look through the windows to check that Willard was not inside.

At first, all he could make out in the darkened interior were flies. Hundreds and hundreds of flies crawling all over the windows and buzzing around the caravan's interior. Something big was lying on the floor.

Joe ran to the campground's office and called the police, who told him to stay well away from the caravan and not to touch anything. Officers would be sent right away. The scene greeting the police that afternoon was horrific. Every surface of the van's interior was splattered with huge amounts of blood, and the stench drove officers out to the fresh air many times during the first scene examination. One officer commented that it looked like the aftermath of a shark-feeding frenzy. Willard's body lay on the floor in a pool of his own blood, the blade of a large knife protruding from his head. The handle had been snapped off and would later be found in a recently vacated cabin.

Not having this information yet, I phoned our local police station and asked to speak with a detective on duty. A deep male voice picked up the call and introduced himself, then asked how he could be of help.

Trying desperately not to cry, I carefully relayed the news we had received the previous day and asked if his station might have received any information about the case.

"Yes," he said. "Bulletins are sent to all stations with this type of case."

"Can you confirm whether Willard's death was murder, please? Or was it a natural death?"

"I'm sorry," he replied, "but I cannot discuss the specifics of the case as it's still under investigation."

"OK, I understand," I said. "Then let me ask you a hypothetical question. If Willard were your father, if you had received the same information that we have, would you conclude that your father had been murdered?"

The detective took a moment to think, then replied, "Yes. Hypothetically, if I had received this information, I would suspect my father had been murdered."

Then he added, "I am so sorry for your loss, Miriam, but there really is nothing more I can help you with at this time."

As hard as it was to hear that, I did have to admit I understood. The investigation was less than 24 hours old. There was still so much information to sift through. And, over the phone, I had no way of proving I was a member of the family and not a reporter trying to get a scoop. I thanked him for his time and hung up.

Our next step was to find out when the coroner would release Willard's body so we could start trying to put a funeral together. This, however, was not going to be easy. Willard's brother Joe kept calling the coroner's office (located in a major city about an hour's drive away) every other day for an update. Then, after ten days, he simply lost patience. Telling them that if Willard was not returned to his family within 24 hours, he would be driving over there to pick up the body himself. "We need to lay my brother to rest," he fumed. "You have kept him long enough. So whatever else you need from the body, get it today! Or I will be there tomorrow."

Within a few hours of that conversation, Joe told us he received a call from the coroner's office asking which funeral home he wanted his brother delivered to. Willard would be returned to us early the next day. Now we could finally lay my father-in-law to rest.

During those ten agonising days, the investigation had come to a quick end when the man responsible for Willard's death was located, along with his missing car and firearm. Thankfully, there was no doubt, as the man confessed openly that he had committed the crime. Over several hours, he went through all the details with the police, who let the family know that a trial would not be required since this man had accepted full responsibility for his actions and understood he would be spending a long time in prison.

Our whole family heaved a huge, collective sigh of relief. Now none of us would have to sit through a trial that could take days or even weeks, listening to all the gory details. We just needed to wait for the sentencing, which would take place in the new year.

Once we had a funeral date, Tom and I could make arrangements to travel half the length of the North Island to attend what was going to be one of the saddest family gatherings imaginable.

I called my mother, who lived about sixty kilometres from where we needed to go.

I was weeping again as I explained what had happened and where we needed to be. "Mum," I stammered. "Can we come and stay with you for a couple of nights, please?"

"Of course, darling. Just get here when you can, and I'll have beds ready for you all. The boys can stay with me while you two attend the funeral."

* * *

We hear a lot about how intrusive the media can be and how, sometimes, facts can be manufactured or ignored completely just to sell papers and gossip magazines. But until then, I had never experienced it for myself.

On the morning we were to travel north, I answered a call at about 7:30 am as we were packing up the last few items for the journey. The male voice on the line stated he was calling from the *Whanganui Chronicle* and was reporting on the murder. He then proceeded to ask if I had a statement he could print.

"Oh, I have a statement for you, alright," I hissed down the phone. "But you won't want to print it. Go away and leave us alone to grieve in peace. Don't you think we have enough to deal with right now?" And with that, I put the receiver back in its cradle. Even in 1986, media intrusion seemed alive and well, even in sleepy little New Zealand.

I do concede that murder was not an everyday occurrence in New Zealand at the time, so it was always going to be front-page news whether we liked it or not. However, in that moment, it made me sick to my stomach that a total stranger would intrude on us so early in the morning just to sensationalise a murder story... our story... our pain.

Who can separate us from the love of Christ?
Can affliction, or distress, or persecution, or famine,
or nakedness, or danger, or sword?
(Romans 8:35 CSB)

2

Grief and Confusion

We decided to stay with Mum for the night and then go on to the funeral in the early morning. That way Tom and I could receive some much-needed support, and Mum would get to spend some time with Alex and James. Living so far away, they didn't get to see a lot of Grandma and Pop. They were excited to go to Grandma's house for a few days but did not fully understand why Tom and I were so sad.

The shift in Tom that I spoke of earlier began to show itself more clearly during the trip north. For the most part, he was quiet throughout the five-hour journey. At the time, I thought, *This whole thing has been such a shock to him. He will be himself again once he has had time to rest and grieve. Give him time. After all, it's a lot to process.*

But once we arrived at my mum's house, and Tom and I had unpacked our luggage and settled the children, he asked if he could please use her phone to call a friend in Auckland. He was happy to pay her for the toll call.

For the next hour, the man I thought I knew poured out his heart to the pastor who would soon marry us and was currently living and working in that city. Although I didn't want to intrude on their conversation, I was hurt that Tom had decided to discuss his pain with Paul rather than me. I had hoped he would, at some time that day, finally open up and share his grief. After all, this was a pain we both felt. Surely sharing it would comfort us both. I was wrong.

Once his time with Paul was over, Tom said he was tired and wanted to take a nap before dinner. He took himself off to the guest room and stayed there for the next couple of hours. As he turned and walked down the hallway, rightly or wrongly, I felt like I had just been slapped in the face. Perhaps Tom didn't see me as being part this situation? Or maybe grief had made me invisible to him in that moment. I tried so hard to push the anger away and not to mind so much since Tom hadn't slept much in the last few days. I wanted to be strong for him, to be the shoulder he could lean on. But where was the shoulder for me to lean on? Not only had I lost Willard, but I felt like Tom had gone too. And then I felt guilty for being so selfish. So many thoughts and emotions rushed around inside me. And in those moments, I could not see God at all. My tears had blinded me to His presence.

While Tom was napping, my mum and I talked quietly over hot coffee. The local evening newspaper was delivered, and the boys eagerly ran to the mailbox to bring it to Grandma. It was laid on the kitchen bench and unfolded, but Mum froze as the front page came into view.

I glanced over her shoulder, wanting to see what had taken her by surprise.

In letters so big, they almost took up the width of the page, the headline read:

"WRONG MAN STABBED."

A gasp of horror escaped me as I took in what I saw. "Tom

can't see this," I whispered to Mum. "Please hide the paper before he gets up. This will devastate him."

Suddenly, I was very, very angry. How did the local newspaper editor imagine that his handiwork would not impact readers who knew Willard? In 1986, New Zealand had a relatively small population (around 3.2 million), and this paper was printed in a town less than an hour from the scene of the crime and had a wide distribution. How did he not know the pain those words would inflict? Would the newspaper sales really outweigh the impact of what he had allowed to go to print? I was quickly learning to understand what media intrusion in people's lives is all about and how comments taken out of context and/or outright lies can be soul-destroying to the ones affected by it.

It turned out that a reporter had interviewed Willard's boss, who, in his shock and grief, said something like: "They must have got the wrong man. Willard had no enemies and wouldn't hurt a fly." That's all it took to turn one bewildered thought into a sensational headline.

Today, that anger is long gone, replaced with the God-given knowledge that our heavenly Father has brought so much good out of our experiences. But still, I wonder if editors would have done the same thing if Willard had been a member of their family. It reminds me that if a headline is sensational, it's probably either only half-true or an outright lie. (To the *honest* newspaper and magazine editors out there – please forgive the generalisation.)

The next morning, Tom and I said goodbye to Mum, hugged Alex and James tightly, and started the journey to Joe's house, where family would already be gathering.

The day had dawned bright and sunny, but my soul could not see the sunshine. As we left the city and drove the state highway through villages and past meadows, trees and farmland, the smell of newly mown hay wafted through the car. Still, all I felt was grey, drab and heavy, like an old musty blanket had been draped over me, and I couldn't see a way out from under it. Tom still wasn't talking to me, and my attempts to start a conversation were met with either one-word answers or a grunt in recognition of my voice. His mind was so far away that I couldn't reach him.

Finally, I blurted out, "I'm hurting too, you know. Can't we please talk? Share our grief? Please, Tom"?

"Not now. Not today," came the curt reply. "Let's just get through this first. Then maybe later." With that, the conversation was over, and the journey continued in almost total silence.

Within an hour, we arrived. Joe met us at the front door with hugs and tears, then ushered us into the living room where Tom's younger sister Kate, brother Keith and sister-in-law Suzette were chatting with other family members, some of whom I had never met.

We all hugged each other tightly. We knew there was nothing we could say that was going to make the day ahead any easier, so we spent time catching up on all the 'other' family news: who had got married recently, who had moved house, who had got a new job or had a baby.

It was during this time that Tom and I suggested to the family that we postpone our wedding. Now did not seem the right moment to be celebrating and seemed disrespectful. Joe, however, objected, saying, "That is the last thing Willard would want. Your wedding must go on just as planned." Other family members joined in, affirming how Willard had been looking forward to the wedding and was excited about coming. He would not have wanted us to change our plans because of him.

Glancing out of the window, I noticed two uniformed police officers chatting with family members on the front lawn. I only briefly wondered why they were there, before Uncle 'Someone' asked where I fitted into the family.

At the appointed time, we all started filing out the door, getting into cars, and sombrely following Joe's car as he led the way to a small, local chapel, where the hearse stood waiting.

I couldn't help noticing those same two police officers were now stationed on each side of the double doors leading into the chapel. *What are they doing here?* I wondered. *Surely they have the man responsible? Why can't they leave us in peace?*

As the service concluded, Tom, Keith, Joe and three others lined up, three-a-side, to carry Willard from the chapel. Row-by-row, friends and family filed out behind them back into the bright sunshine. Now it was getting really warm.

Stepping past the two police officers, now standing to attention like carved wooden sentries at the doorway, I began to feel like we had not been told something. Why were they still there?

Back into a now hot car, lights on, we found our place in a line of more than twenty vehicles heading for the graveyard. Tom managed to find a park under some trees, and I knew I would be very grateful to him when the time came to leave. This day was going to get a lot hotter. Thank goodness I had dressed lightly.

Wandering up the cemetery driveway, past neatly-manicured lawns between rows and rows of headstones, we joined our family gathered around a yawning, six-foot hole to bid farewell to Willard for the last time. I lifted my gaze towards the faces around me for just a moment, and there again saw the two police officers, standing to the rear of the gathered mourners, hands respectfully clasped in front, heads bowed. I was confused at the intrusion, and even more so when I found that they had followed us back to the house. This time, their presence got the better of me.

As Suzette and I walked up the driveway toward the front door, I asked her (without lowering my voice), "Why are they still hanging about? Is there something we don't know? Or are they expecting another person of interest to be among us today? What are they looking for?"

Suzette shrugged. "I don't know. I thought the case was closed, but they have been hanging around all day. Who knows what they want."

Now we had their attention, and one officer wandered up to us.

"Ladies," he smiled, a little embarrassed. "Sorry to have spooked you today. My buddy and I were Willard's friends. We used to go fishing together a lot. We just wanted to pay our respects to a mate."

Suddenly I felt like such a fool and very ashamed of myself. I tried to apologise for our remarks, but the young man said he understood that we were all feeling the strain today. It was OK. They had not been offended. (Note to self: Never presume anything.)

* * *

In our darkest moments, all human beings tend to imagine the worst possible scenario. We think of all the things that *could* go wrong and focus on the storm raging around us, instead of raising our eyes above the waves. If I had just kept my eyes firmly focused on Him, I would have found Jesus waiting, his hand extended, ready for me to reach out and hold on.

Sometimes, holding on is all we can make ourselves do – allowing Him to embrace us till the storm passes. In the months following the funeral, I was holding on for dear life. Looking back now, I have to ask myself how I did that. What had changed in me that kept my head above the waves of grief?

There is no simple answer to those questions except that I had, little by little, become very aware of the presence of the Holy Spirit. He wasn't doing anything spectacular or earth-shattering. He was just there, giving me the strength to put one foot in front of the other, holding me together, one moment at a time. Prayer became what I can only describe as a 'pleading fest'. At least, that's how it felt and sounded to me at the time. 2 Corinthians 12:9 (CSB) says: *My grace is sufficient for you, for my power is perfected in weakness.* So, I gave Him my weakness, one day at a time.

Returning home, we tried to pick up the pieces of our lives. Tom went back to work. The boys went back to school. And I was suddenly the busiest housewife on the block. We now had just a few days to complete wedding plans. I was doing most of the catering myself, so spent many hours in the kitchen. Mum would arrive in a day or two and would be keen to help, but somehow, I felt that if I could just keep busy, I wouldn't have to think. So, I ironed and re-ironed my wedding suit. I called the florist to check what time the flowers would arrive. I called the suit hire store to check they had the order for the three suits correct – one each for Tom, Alex and James.

My very dear friend Patricia visited on the Wednesday before the wedding and we talked about how the last weeks had changed Tom. I felt sure that getting married was still the right thing to do. I could not abandon Tom when he needed me the most and was determined to give the man I loved all the support and love he would need to work through his grief. Patricia decided I should spend the night before the big day at her house, where we could pamper ourselves. It would, she said, *make* me relax.

I remember the flowers arriving at the house just after my return on Saturday morning. Looking through them, we noticed we had not cancelled Willard's buttonhole flower. At the wedding reception later that day, we laid it on the plate that had been put where Willard was to sit, as a tribute to the man whose light had been extinguished too soon.

In the days, weeks and months that followed, most of my energy was spent caring for Tom and the boys. Children need stability and routine, and that is what I focused on. School, homework, weekend sports games, anything and everything to keep them busy and keep me from thinking. Only in prayer did I find the peace I needed.

Many times, Tom and I tried to address the guilt and anger we both felt. And many times, we just didn't. The household dynamic had changed completely. Tom and I were just going through the motions, smiling with and for the boys but finding no joy or loveliness in our lives. We still loved each other very much, but in spite of that, or maybe because of that, we tiptoed around each other, trying not to offend, trying to be strong for each other, trying to *make* life normal again. We wanted desperately for it all to have been a bad dream where we could wake up and go back to the way things were before – before that day in the caravan park, before this horror began, before we stopped talking.

If only we hadn't stopped talking.

*Come quickly to help me,
my Lord and my Saviour.*
(Psalm 38:22 NIV)

3

Jesus Came to Visit

In early 1987, the man who killed Willard (I will call him Daniel) was sentenced to life in prison, with a non-parole period of eight years. His future, for the next eight years at least, was certain.

As his family were in Auckland, Daniel would spend those years at Pāremoremo Correctional Facility and was admitted to the maximum-security unit that same month.

Our life sentence, however, had just begun. We would live with the heartbreaking aftermath for the rest of our lives.

Almost overnight, Tom and I had become two very different people. Right from the first day, Tom had shut down completely as he tried to work his way through his grief. I remember a comment in the book *Men Are from Mars, Women Are from Venus*. It said something like: "When men need to work out a deep or personal problem, they generally crawl into their cave and slam the door till the problem is either solved or has gone away." And, in essence, that is exactly what Tom did. I believe something died in him, and to this day, I'm not sure the door was ever fully opened again. This means that I can only continue this story from my own perspective, as I often had no idea what Tom was thinking or feeling.

I kept myself busy with everyday chores to emotionally

avoid the crushing grief. Not only had *we* lost Willard, but it felt like I had also lost Tom. I loved this man desperately, to the point that I could not imagine my life without him. But he had become unreachable to me now. And each time we tried to talk about anything even close to the subject of Willard, it was like walking on quicksand. We still attended church every Sunday. We still had a study group at our home each week. But over time, I began to experience very real spiritual doubts. How could a loving God have let this senseless killing happen? And why was the man I loved shutting me out of his life? As much as I tried, I thought I would never understand it.

And, of course, the enemy was taking full advantage of that grief and confusion, planting doubts, whispering nasty lies into an already broken heart, sowing seeds of discord in our relationship.

Trying to sweep rampant and sometimes unreasonable emotions under the carpet was no longer working for me. I was being bombarded with them day and night. Those seeds of discord were beginning to take root in our hearts. The distance between us was steadily growing. I was not sleeping well. I was often up during the night, talking to God and praying for answers, sometimes arguing the point with Him. One moment, I hated what He had allowed to happen, and the next, I was begging for forgiveness for that hatefulness while doubting my own faith.

Then, late one night, after much praying and questioning, I was granted a wondrous vision or dream. Jesus had me stand in our darkened midnight home, looking out the front window and staring at the damp pavement, lit only by a streetlight a few houses down from ours; I begged the Lord, "Jesus... if you are real, Lord, if you are really there, *please*, show me!"

Slowly, the darkness outside the window began to show the softest glow of light. It was just a tiny bit at first, but it steadily grew brighter, like an approaching vehicle far off in the distance, inching closer, until the light became a brilliant spot, lighting up our whole front yard.

As my eyes adjusted to the brilliance, I could make out the shape of a man, dimly at first but slowly taking shape more and more as he drew closer. The figure was walking toward me, seeming to walk right through the hedge and onto our lawn without hesitation. Suddenly, my soul recognised Him. My Lord and Saviour, Jesus Christ, Emmanuel, stood just a few feet from the window with a gentle smile on His face and arms reaching toward me as if waiting for an embrace. He answered me, saying, "Miriam, I am here. Believe."

At once, I was back in my bed, staring at the ceiling, trying to explain to myself what I had just seen, but there was only one explanation. Jesus had come to my house. Come to tell me, to show me that He is *real* and that He loves me. All doubt was gone. I was finally sure that He was and is my Lord. My king. Son of the living God. And my best friend. In that moment, I knew I belonged to Him and He to me.

When morning came, I was so excited as I tried to explain to Tom what I had seen, but he never said if it impacted him. He wasn't saying much at all about his faith at that stage. It was almost as if he hadn't heard or understood what I was saying. Great damage had already been done in our marriage, almost before it had begun, but we had no idea how to mend it or even where to begin, so it was never addressed in any meaningful way. *Keep calm and carry on* seemed to be the way of it now. But nothing will ever make me forget the wonderful night when Jesus came to visit me at home, of the peace and hope that was born anew in me. The soft glow of His presence remained with me for many weeks.

Within twelve months of that beautiful night, we moved to the Bay of Plenty to take up the opportunity of working on a dairy farm as part-time milkers in exchange for rent. Or rather, I did most of the milking so Tom could take up work and provide us with an income. Free rent is great, but we still needed to eat and pay the utility bills. Things between us improved a little as we worked together well, sharing the load and learning to laugh again.

But real intimacy was still a very rare thing. It seems the enemy had been lying to Tom too – twisting his faith both in the Lord and in himself. Turning something wonderful and righteous into something he suddenly found dirty and shameful and planting in his soul the notion that physical love, even with his wife, was a sin and must not happen again. So, we were housemates, on good terms, co-parenting two boys who, thankfully, had no idea anything was amiss. I could see Tom was struggling, but nothing I did or said dissuaded him from this current, hurtful path. It was clear the enemy had his hooks in good and deep. And again, hard work filled the void. I milked cows, fed calves, raised pigs for the table and gardened in between working night shifts at a local retirement home – such a busy routine leaves little time for wallowing in self-pity.

During the farming years, we attended a local Baptist church where we both became very involved in the fellowship. Tom was in the sound booth, and I joined the music group. Sundays became a time of refuge for me. Being in that little chapel, singing my heart out for the Lord (as King David said it, *making a joyful noise*) was my happy place. Being a part of a like-minded, Jesus-following, loving community filled up all the dark spaces with light and joy. I was even working part-time in the church office and was later voted onto the deacon's board and felt blessed and very privileged to serve. Pouring so much of my energy into church business started a healing within me. I began to feel my Jesus stepping closer to me, holding on tight to my fragile, brittle spirit, whispering His love into my soul and catching me every time I fell. And that was often, I confess.

Peace I leave with you; my peace I give you.
I do not give to you as the world gives.
Do not let your hearts be troubled and do not be afraid.
(John 14:27 NIV)

4

The Lesson: Forgiveness

It was now five years since we lost Willard, and the unforgiveness and unresolved grief, guilt and anger that had inched into our lives finally reared its ugly head in my heart, carefully hidden from the children. It was time to do something about it. But what?

I honestly don't remember how the most important conversation of our lives started, but we finally discussed the issue of forgiveness. It dawned on us that our inability to forgive Daniel, or ourselves, for the way we dealt (or hadn't dealt) with the aftermath of Willard's death was not affecting Daniel at all. He went about his daily prison routine, never knowing that our world was silently crumbling around us.

We attended a weekly Bible study evening, and it was during one of these study nights that God led us to Genesis 42-45 – the story of Joseph, son of Jacob – and how this now-mighty man of God and governor of Egypt had to learn to forgive the brothers who had sold him into slavery many years earlier.

As we went through the story together, we came to understand Joseph had experienced many of the same emotions Tom and I had been grappling with for years. And just like us, Joseph had decided to do something about it. Forgiving this man for what he had done had never crossed our minds... but it should have...

Genesis 45:2 says that during this time, Joseph wept so loudly that both the Egyptian servants and Pharaoh's household heard it, showing us that Joseph's pain, after all those years, was as deep and raw as our own.

As we read on through that chapter, we see Joseph drawing his brothers to him, telling them who he was and asking them not to grieve or be angry with themselves because all that they did was done for a reason. He then told them to return to their father, gather up their family and return to live with him in Egypt so he could take care of them. *This must be what it truly means to forgive. Forgive as God forgives.*

Once we had decided to forgive, God gently told us He wanted to lead our family through that process. He would be there, step by agonising step, and would stand beside us all the way. He would open doors that might stand in our way. And He meant that. Our Lord is not a God of lies or deception but of truth, clarity, mercy and endless faithfulness. If we were willing to commit to following this through, so was He. All we had to do was trust. Sounds easy, doesn't it? But the path ahead was anything but.

How glad I am that our Father does not show us tomorrow. I am so grateful that the future remains a mystery. For if we knew the cost, would we dare to tread the path He has laid out for us? I'm not sure I would have volunteered for this journey had I known the toll it would take. But looking back from the safe distance of more than 35 years, I can say with absolute honesty that there simply was no other way. I can now recognise the many times Jesus was standing by my side and how often He carried me through the very darkest days.

We soon realised we were not going to get away with simply saying, "I forgive him". Oh no! There would be much more to this than we could have imagined – much, much more.

Forgiveness is not just a 'feel-good' thing. Matthew 6:14,15 (NIV) says, *For if you forgive other people when they sin against you, your heavenly Father will also forgive you. But if you do not forgive others their sins, your Father will not forgive your sins.*

My mother's younger brother, Michael Bensley, was a pastor and the gentlest, most Spirit-filled man I ever knew. His love for Jesus glowed and radiated from him every day. This dear man suffered with a dreadful stutter every day of his life, until the moment he started to preach or minister to others. Each time, the Spirit took him by the hand, and the stutter miraculously vanished. Just being in his company was a living lesson in grace and holy humility. And it was this wonderful uncle that we talked to about how to begin putting things right. How to be obedient to what God was asking us to do: to forgive, heal, and finally move on from this monstrous tragedy that was consuming our lives like a cancer.

My uncle asked us to be open to the idea of what real forgiveness might look like in this situation. He suggested visiting Daniel in prison and discussing what had happened in 1986. Tom reluctantly agreed to the idea of contacting Daniel, but while he agreed that forgiving was the right thing to do, he stopped short of wanting to make first contact. Fear was holding him back, so he asked if I would go up first and test the waters. Then, if it went well, he would come with me the second time. My dear uncle immediately suggested he could come with me the first time, in Tom's place.

From this experience, I can tell you plainly that *'devil-planted fear'* is a truly terrible thing to experience, and even more terrible to watch as it takes hold of a loved one. It saps you of all spiritual strength and common sense. The small child inside you suddenly appears, trembling, trying to hide behind others. Wallowing in self-pity that is used as an excuse for bad behaviour towards family and friends, leaves the body weak and the spirit wide open to attack. That attack took a huge toll on Tom. It stole his confidence and was hard to see in my big, strong husband.

Proverbs 3:5 (NIV) says: *Trust in the Lord with all your heart and lean not on your own understanding.* I confess that I had no clue what I was stepping into. But with Uncle Mike's support and the very clear knowledge that this was what God was asking of me, I was about to do the bravest thing I think I have ever done.

The first step was to call the prison and speak with the chaplain. He would be the one to know what I needed to do in order to visit with Daniel. Over the phone, I explained who I was and what Uncle Mike and I wanted to do. The chaplain was understandably surprised that a murder victim's family would even want to make eye contact with the one responsible but was keen to help us make it happen. He agreed to arrange our visit for the following week and said he would let Daniel's unit manager know we were coming so officers could have Daniel available for our visit.

How grateful I was not to be making this trip alone. As a pastor, Uncle Mike had been in all sorts of demanding situations during his many years of service and had the kind of experience I would need at my side when I finally came face-to-face with Daniel. And I confess, the child in me felt safe knowing that wherever Mike went, God would surely be. That's just how it was with my uncle.

However, in what I can only describe as childish rebellion, I thought, *No rush. He is a murderer, after all. He can wait, right?* He might, but could we?

The following Thursday morning, Uncle Mike picked me up from my home, and we drove to Pāremoremo Prison. My uncle could see I was nervous, so kept the conversation light. We must have talked about anything and everything *except* Pāremoremo or Daniel. At some point during the trip, however, it suddenly occurred to me that I was about to sit down with the man who savagely took Willard's life. My mouth went dry, and my hands were damp as I thought about everything I wanted to say and all the things that could go wrong. Was Daniel as nervous as I was about this meeting? Would he even see me? Would we even be allowed in?

* * *

We've all seen murderers portrayed on television and in the movies. The typical, evil-looking, tattooed bad guy with a permanent sneer on his face. Have you ever thought about sitting down for a chat with one over a hot coffee? Have you ever wondered how that might go? Nail biting. Toe curling. Hand ringing. Blood-curdling. That's how it goes. Believe me, I was completely unsettled. But my wonderful Uncle was going to be there, and I remembered 1 John 4:18 (NIV), which says that God's *perfect love drives out fear*. And Psalm 9:10 (TLB) says *All those who know your mercy, Lord, will count on you for help. For you have never yet forsaken those who trust you.*

Minute by minute, I was learning what trusting Him meant for me. But letting go of control altogether was never going to be easy. This one lesson would be the hardest for me and is something I still struggle with. I would be OK, I decided, if I could just make those butterflies in my stomach fly in formation! I reminded myself that deep down, I knew that in Christ Jesus, all things are possible, including this. Jesus, Uncle Mike and me – together, we made a mighty combination. Together, we had the strength. And we would go through with this day's work together.

Now, here's where the fun started. We arrived at Pāremoremo right on time. We parked the car and made our way across the lot to the gate. We were then escorted to the office, where our arrival was announced. But no one had passed the message to the unit officers that we were coming, so Daniel had not been brought in from his work detail. Someone called the Chaplain, who confessed he had been so busy that he had forgotten all about our visit, but that permission had been given. Well, at least Daniel had not gone through days of nervous uncertainty while he awaited our arrival. He would not have had the opportunity to talk himself out of attending this meeting. I was grateful for that. I was not sure why yet, but I was grateful.

An officer was dispatched to go and fetch Daniel and bring him back to the visiting room. A second officer escorted Uncle Mike and I to that same room, then stationed himself at the exit of this large, uninviting hall-sized space furnished with rows of tables and hard wooden chairs to accommodate family members on visiting days.

While we waited, Uncle Mike sat with his hand in mine, and together, we prayed. Mike's voice was quiet as he gently asked God for strength and mercy as the three of us met for the first time. I then asked, for what must have been the millionth time, for the Lord to be with us and to stay close by until it was time to go. We were desperate for this to go well but didn't really know what to expect except that we would not be alone. We both felt that Jesus would be there, standing with us, just as He promised.

On his way to the visiting room, Daniel was simply told that a member of his victim's family was waiting to speak with him. Understandably, he was as nervous of me as I was of him. He may have been expecting the worst possible scenario, just as I had. He may have wondered what on earth the family wanted of him after all these years.

And then the door opened, and there he was... A very tall, brown-skinned, doe-eyed teddy bear of a man. Nothing like the TV murderer I had envisioned. And yes, he was clearly very unsettled by our presence.

I rose to my feet and extended my hand. "Good morning," I said. "Do you know who I am?"

Daniel did not see my hand, his strong face going pale as he answered, "No. Not really, except that you are related to the man I killed."

"My name is Miriam Murphy," I said. "And your victim was my father-in-law." As the remaining blood drained, his already pale face now turned ashen. And at once I regretted that my words had come out sounding so harsh. I hadn't meant them to. So I stumbled on: "Look, I'm not here to cause you any trouble. In fact, I came to tell you that you are forgiven."

There. It was out. I had spoken the words, so there was no going back. God had just committed me to seeing it through to an ending that *He* had planned.

By this point, I was already fighting back tears, so I introduced Uncle Mike, and we three settled into seats, Mike and I on one side of the table and Daniel facing us from the other. Soon enough, the conversation began but skirted around the real reason for this meeting. We spoke about Daniel's work at the prison. About the weather and about anything and everything except Willard. So, my wonderful Uncle took charge and reached across the table. He took Daniel's and my hands in his, and each of us suddenly felt a shift in the room. The Holy Spirit was there, moving between us. Touching us. Working with us and through us. In that moment, God's promise to me was kept.

After a short prayer, Mike stood and walked to the doorway to chat with the guard still stationed there. For a second, I wondered why he would do that, but then relaxed a little, knowing there were still *three* at the table. Mike was close enough to watch over me but far enough not to hear us. Now it was just the Holy Spirit, Daniel, and me. This was a situation I never dreamed I would be in, but as we began to talk and the discomfort faded, Daniel told me he was raised in a very strict Jehovah's Witness home, so understood the concept of forgiveness, but had never personally experienced it in this way. No one had said "I forgive you" to him for something this big. He was truly amazed that God, or anyone, could ever forgive him. Some members of his family had not. In all his years behind bars, his father had never visited. Not even once.

As the time passed, we talked a lot about forgiveness and what that might mean to us all. I told him about how the story of Joseph and his brothers had led us to understand God's wish to end our suffering, and his. He wanted healing for us all. I felt like we could start by getting to know each other a little better, and that Tom had decided he may also make the trip next time if Daniel was OK with that.

That day, Daniel confessed there had been times over the past years he had seriously contemplated ending his own life. The guilt of what he had done and the grief for the self he had lost had often overwhelmed him. So yes, he was very

OK with the idea of meeting Tom. The two men had a lot to say to each other. There did need to be a healing. So, I thought, *the enemy has been busy here, too. Willard's life has already been destroyed, and now the devil wants Daniel's as well. But with God's help, maybe that could be prevented.* The hour ended too soon. Daniel and I had sat and listened to each other and wept together. Now, as we stood, Daniel reached for my hand across the table and squeezed it tight. This big, soft brown teddy bear of a man walked around to me, took me in his arms and hugged me tightly. There I was, wrapped in the same arms that had stabbed, hacked and slashed my father-in-law to death. And in his embrace, I was not afraid.

Three weeks later, Tom and I returned to that same visiting room. And this time, it was me who walked away from the table, leaving the two men alone together. And just like Uncle Mike, I was far enough not to hear them, but close enough to... I really was not sure what I would do if things went badly. These two had to work it out for themselves, but the body language told me that like two angry bobcats, they were circling, sizing each other up, each trying to work out the measure of the man across the table, looking for a way past the armour. From where I was standing, I could not tell whether this meeting would work or not, but I could trust that at least God knew, and for now, that had to be enough.

This behaviour was repeated at the next visit a month later. By Tom's third visit, however, the ice had begun to melt a little. Only a little. Now I thought it would be OK for me to stay at the table and join the conversation. Well, at least each man had decided he would not be eaten by the other. It was a start.

Tom and Daniel took their time working out their differences and finding common ground, sharing with each other the things they agreed on, and carefully debating the things they didn't. And with each successive visit, their relationship and spiritual connection developed and grew into a deep and genuine friendship. It seemed to me that both men were truly learning Joseph's lesson. Tom was slowly letting go of the pain that had bound his heart for so long. Together, these two men held the key to healing each other. I thank God for the wonderful work He was doing in their lives, and in mine too.

*...being confident of this,
that he who began a good work in you will carry it
on to completion until the day of Christ Jesus.*
(Philippians 1:6 NIV)

5

A Loving Ministry

Back at home, we were asked by the church leadership to accept a position as 'house parents' in a new project. 'Te Whare Manaaki' (Te Whare – meaning the home or house; and Manaaki – meaning to support, take care of, give hospitality to, protect and show respect and generosity) was to be opened as a halfway house for at-risk teenagers. We accepted the mission gladly.

A very large four-bedroom villa was chosen in town which, after cleaning and redecorating, could accommodate up to fourteen kids. The house had a huge, closed-in, secure veranda covering two sides of the building. Here, we could accommodate four, on two sets of bunk-beds with room for dressers. Another *BOYS* room held five. The *GIRLS* room housed up to four, with room for up to two more in a small bedroom just off the dining room. Then there were my two boys plus us.

My sister Christine travelled from Taranaki to help with the big move, and amid all the stacked boxes, noise and mess, we welcomed our first resident as we ourselves were moving in. A big, strong lad who was happy to help with heavy boxes. What an adventure this was going to be.

Our large dining table could seat up to eighteen and often did, as our residents' friends came to visit and sometimes needed a helping hand (talk about the Walton family).

I was very quickly christened with the title of 'Aunty Mum', and I really enjoyed teaching my gang, male and female alike, how to keep house and make a meal out of leftovers. I quickly became adept at making a casserole in the big roasting dish, since that was our biggest oven dish. Supermarket day was usually a two-person job since most weeks we filled two trolleys and sometimes three. There were always willing helpers to come give me a hand if Tom was not about; however, this meant that now and then, extra 'special treat items' would find their way into the trolleys. I had to be very vigilant at the checkout as, more than once, someone was sent to return chocolate or cookies to the shelves.

We informed each member of our household why we were making regular trips to Pāremoremo, and Tom explained to them the importance of forgiving each other when we made mistakes, even referring to Joseph's story to make his point. We would often return from a daytime prison visit to a barrage of questions. Everyone wanted to know how Daniel was doing. Had we told him about them? When would we be going again? Did we think he would be able to visit Te Whare Manaaki and meet them when he was released? We said we did not know if that would be allowed in the short term, as we thought there might be a probationary time for a while. He may not be allowed to travel far at first. A great debate was had about the 'unfairness' of that. Tom just smiled and said we would all have to wait and see. I just wanted to see Daniel free.

Our youngest resident at Te Whare Manaaki was a two-day-old baby girl, Nikki, who came to us directly from the maternity unit with her 16-year-old mother, who had been arrested for packing hospital property into her bag. The sweet teenager had panicked on the day she was to leave hospital. Not knowing anything about Te Whare Manaaki and whether we would take care of her and her tiny daughter, and with no money, she wondered how she would buy the things she would need. The police were given our contact details and let us know when this young mum would need to appear in court.

About three weeks after their arrival, we almost lost little Nikki to cot death. But God was onto it. Wee Nikki was being settled for the night by her visiting 18-year-old aunt, but within just a few minutes, her tiny, limp and grey body was carried to me by the panicked young woman.

"Aunty Mum, Aunty Mum!" she yelped. "Something is wrong with baby. She's not moving!"

I took this tiny wee girl from her aunty and put her on the floor, placing two shaky fingers in the middle of her chest. I needed to do CPR on a three-week-old child, but knew that if I used too much pressure, I could break something, and if I breathed too much air into her lungs, I could kill her. "God, help me!" Suddenly, the house was in an uproar, as if that little girl belonged to all of us.

Nikki's daddy was visiting and was with Tom and the other young men playing pool in the garage. Someone yelled for help, and both men raced into the house. "Call an ambulance. Now!" I gasped between breaths. "And tell them it's for a baby who needs oxygen. They will need an infant mask."

Nikki's dad knelt on the floor next to me, desperate to do something, anything, but not knowing what. Panic was beginning to take hold, and he kept reaching for his daughter and then pulling his hand away. Daddys are meant to know how to make things better, to do the right thing for their children, but just now, there was nothing he could do, and he knew it. His young face looked totally desolate and desperate.

Tom placed a hand on this very young dad's arm and lifting him gently from the floor just held him, speaking quietly. In that moment, I was so very thankful for my husband who, in comforting another, had also given me comfort and the room I needed to concentrate on the tiny body in front of me, while the two sisters clung tightly to each other and to other residents around the room staring in horror at the scene unfolding on the floor.

It only took about ten minutes for the ambulance to arrive, but it felt like forever. All our teens were talking at once, some weeping, all in shock, until paramedics were at last shown into the dining room where I was still trying to keep Nikki alive. How relieved I was that they were there to take over this task, which they did very quickly, and soon she and her mum were placed in the ambulance and whisked off to the hospital. I had been so afraid that I might have done something wrong and caused her harm.

I had been partway through a first aid course required for us to continue in our roles as house parents. The next morning, I called my tutor and explained what had happened the night before. I thanked her for the CPR lesson.

"No, Miriam," she whispered down the line. "That's next week's lesson, and I think you just passed it!" Wow... Thank you, dear Lord. I could not have done it without you.

In little more than a week from that dreadful night, we had our wee Nikki back with us, so well and happy that no one would ever guess at the terror of that night. The mood in our house was one of universal joy and thankfulness. Nikki really did belong to all of us.

Our oldest resident was a beautiful eighty-something-year-old Māori lady who taught me such a lot about acceptance and grace, being content with what we are given, without complaint, and dignity in adversity.

Dear Molly, God love her, said we were a blessing to her, but the truth is she blessed us every day with her sharp wit, ready smile and infectious laugh. Her sensible, no-nonsense Māori wisdom could only be learned through living. I could not have passed that sort of gift on to our young people at the time, but for the few months Molly was with us, she happily became a 'Nana' to all, and I was delighted to surprise her one day with a muttonbird. This is a Māori term for the Sooty Shearwater bird and is a delicacy that roosts on the mostly uninhabited islands surrounding Stewart Island (referred to as the Muttonbird or Titi Islands) and traditionally harvested during April and May. These birds, I am told, are delicious and can sometimes be hard to buy. I knew Molly was particularly fond of them so, for her birthday, I placed a special order with our local butcher as a gift. She wagged her finger at me for making such a fuss of her; however, she was soon in the kitchen teaching me the 'correct' way to cook a muttonbird.

When the time came for Molly to move on, I was genuinely sorry to see her go. For such a little lady, she had left huge footprints behind her and was deeply missed by us all.

We made many trips to visit Daniel during our time at Te Whare Manaaki. Every few months, the prison would hold a 'family day'. These would usually involve inmate's families coming in with baskets filled with picnic food. The baskets were carefully searched for contraband before each family was allowed to enter an open yard to join their loved ones for the day.

Along one side of the enclosed yard, there would usually be a display of some of the beautiful artwork produced by the men.

These might be paintings, wood carvings, or flaxwork. Each piece was carefully placed, ready to be presented to a parent or sibling.

We were the only ones to come to share these 'family' picnics with Daniel, so we (Alex and James included) were treated as family, welcomed and respected as much as any other family member. Soon enough, it became clear to inmates and families alike who we were. Alex and James were treated with gentle respect by all as the story of our attachment to Daniel quickly spread after our first family visit.

Two family day trips have remained very clear in my memory. On one occasion, I sat on a bench seat between Tom and the unit manager, watching a game of touch rugby in the yard. There were my two sons, aged about 10 and 12 at the time, amongst all the inmates: murderers, thieves, rapists, fraudsters and gang members. All those people that 'decent society' would put away as write-offs. And here I was, a mother, not the least bit concerned for my children's safety.

For a moment, I questioned my mothering instincts, asking myself, "How is this OK?" But then I remembered that God, Tom, and Daniel were keeping a very close eye on my boys. Nothing was going to happen to them. And anyway, they were having the time of their lives. I admit there are not many mothers who would have felt as confident as I did that day, but it seemed that even the other inmates treated the two boys with a special kind of reverence, knowing who they were and what it meant to Daniel to have them there. I will forever be grateful to God for teaching me about the way Jesus loved, giving care and respect to the unlovely. That same care and respect shown on a rugby field between prison inmates and two young boys will stay with me always.

The second very special family day was for a very different reason. The picnic and games were over, and families were beginning to pack up and drift away one by one. Daniel asked if we would like to wander over to his cabin area so we could sit in the shade and talk privately for a while, away from all the noise and chatter. A little lemonade was left in our basket, and this was shared out between us. We sat, enjoying our last few minutes together; we three adults in deep conversation while the boys entertained themselves on the lawn. Suddenly, without warning, Daniel got up from his seat, walked over to James and took a firm grip on his hand. He gave me a quick wink, then marched James up to the wire fence. There, he leaned in close, and quietly, but in no uncertain terms, warned my son about the need to stay well away from anything that might result in him ending up on the wrong side of the fence for anything other than a visit. Then he simply stepped back to rejoin Tom and I in the shade as if nothing had happened.

Clearly Daniel had seen something developing in James's behaviour over the years that concerned him deeply enough to do something about keeping this youngster on the straight and narrow. It worked. Much later, James said that, during his late teenage years, opportunities had arisen that could have landed him in a lot of trouble with the police. Each time, however, James said he could feel the proximity of that wire fence and would hear Daniel's words in his ear. And each time, he stopped and walked away. Thank you, Lord. And thank you, Daniel. I will forever be grateful to God for that intervention. I believe it may have saved my rebellious son's life more than once.

It was during this visit that I mentioned to Daniel that I felt God was asking me to write our story down, to share with others the lessons we had learned and to encourage others to seek out the miracles of forgiveness for themselves. As this was also Daniel's story, I felt that he needed to be completely comfortable with me doing that, provided I changed all names, so he would never be stopped in the street. Daniel happily agreed to the idea.

*We know that all things work together for
the good of those who love God,
who are called according to his purpose.*
(Romans 8:28 CSB)

6

Miracles

Our visits to Pāremoremo continued for about three years, and our lives just kept getting busier. Tom was in great demand with his job and worked long hours. The boys were involved with after-school and weekend sports, as well as youth group activities alongside some of our young people. And my involvement with the church and halfway house kept me very busy.

We could see that our personal relationship with Daniel continued to be of great interest to our young residents at Te Whare Manaaki and we would share updates with them as often as possible. In fact, one of our special young ladies had developed such an interest that we even included her in one of our visits.

Ruby had called us 'Dad' and 'Aunty Mum' from almost her first day with us and was particularly close to Tom. I thought it was good for her to have a strong father figure in her life, as with all our residents, seeing how we behaved as parents would be a good example for them to emulate as they grew and became parents themselves. Well, that was the plan and why we became house parents.

I was alone at home one afternoon when the phone rang. An operator asked if I would accept a collect call from Daniel. This had never happened before, so I was afraid something was wrong. "Yes, of course," I stammered.

Almost before the operator connected us, Daniel was already speaking, very quickly, like an excited child. "Miriam, it's happening!"

"Daniel, what's happening? Is everything all right?"

"Yeah, yeah, everything is great. I have a parole hearing in three weeks! Can you both be here? Please say you will be here." (That would place the hearing date in mid-November 1994.)

Without hesitation, I said, "Yes, of course we will be there. Money is tight, so we will have to juggle it a bit, but we *will* be there somehow, I promise."

Hanging up the phone from that call, my first thought was, *Oh boy! How in the world are we going to manage this?* When I said we had very little money, I was serious. I am sure that most parents know when raising children, after you've deducted the essentials, there is not much left over to cover unexpected trips, especially when there is only one wage coming into the household. It seemed that Alex and James were growing up fast and getting taller by the minute. They needed *something* new or replaced almost every other week. So, that evening, Tom and I got on our knees to ask God's help. We knew instinctively that He would want to finish the work He had started in us, and that without His intervention, we could not find even enough money to fill the car with petrol.

Our loving Father had it all worked out. The first miracle happened the very next morning. When Tom got to work, he spoke with his boss, Cole, about what would happen in three weeks and to ask if it was possible to have that day off. Cole was not a Christian but had been hearing all about our prison visits for some time. He openly admitted he couldn't understand why on earth we would want to do this for a killer, but since we were committed to it, he would give Tom the day off with full pay.

Tom was really excited for the day to be over so he could come home and tell me all about it.

That same morning, I went into the church office to talk with the pastor who had supported us in prayer throughout the last few years of our journey. When he heard of the phone call and our impending trip to Pāremoremo, he smiled and instinctively said, "Right, how can I help? What do you need? Do you have money for petrol? Wait here, I'll be right back." He then rose from his chair and rushed out of the office. I sat there stunned when, after a few minutes, our pastor returned with an envelope filled with enough money for the trip and a bite to eat along the way. Wow, was I going to have a wonderful story to tell Tom when he got home.

That evening, Tom strode through the kitchen door with a big grin on his face and a tale to tell about the boss who believed he was crazy but would support him anyway. I could hardly sit still while he told me how hard it had been for Cole to understand that we could possibly forgive the man who had taken Willard's life and then why we would want to attend a parole hearing, not to try to keep Daniel locked up for the rest of his life, but to ask for his release sooner rather than later.

Finally, it was my turn to share the rest of God's miracle and to place the pastor's money gift on the table. Tom's face lit up with the smile that I loved so much. God's first miracle was done. We would be at that parole hearing. Now we knew for sure this was exactly what we were meant to be doing. Psalm 136:3 says, *Give thanks to the Lord of lords, for His steadfast love endures forever.* We truly have an amazing heavenly Father who just loves to surprise His children with unexpected blessings right when we need them the most.

And so it was that on the appointed day, we arrived at

Pāremoremo and pulled into the parking lot of the maximum-security section of the prison. Established in 1968, it is described as New Zealand's only specialist maximum-security prison unit. We had never been there before because Daniel had been moved from there well before we met, but this was where the hearing was taking place.

Even from the outside, it was plain to see that this place really was something else, quite different from the minimum-security section we had become accustomed to. Here, there were double-wire fences topped with tight rings of razor wire. I was completely intimidated even before a burly uniformed officer opened the first gate and escorted us to the reception area.

"This is going to be interesting," Tom whispered as we walked through the entrance. To our right was an office, closed off except for chest-high sliding glass panels that allowed another officer to speak with us. This gentleman was shorter than the last and spoke with a strong Welsh accent. Upon giving our names, he began searching his paperwork for any mention of us and our permission to be there. After several frustrating moments, he covered the papers and announced that we would not be allowed to attend the hearing since our names were not on his list.

"List! What list? No one ever mentioned that we needed to be on a list." Tom was shaken by this development and didn't mind showing it.

Holding tightly to Tom's hand, I gently explained how we came to be there. "Is there anything you can do to help us, please? We have come such a long way, and Daniel is expecting us."

"Well, I don't know." The officer stopped, thought for a while, and said, "I tell you what. I can't let you in, but I can make a call to the Board. Maybe they will allow you to visit Daniel for a few minutes after the hearing is over. At least you would get to see him before you go home." And with that, he marched off, leaving us in an otherwise empty waiting room.

Tom and I started pacing back and forth across the small room, talking to God. "Lord," I said. "We know you didn't bring us all this way just so we could sit in this room and wait. Father, you opened prison doors for Simon Peter. If you really want us in that hearing, please open these doors for us now." Tom joined in, and together we laid the whole situation in God's hands.

Remember earlier I mentioned that God would open doors? I kid you not, less than ten minutes had gone by when the Welsh officer was back. And he didn't look happy.

"Well," he announced. "I don't know who you people are, but you must have friends in very high places. There will be another guard here shortly to escort you to the parole hearing."

Friends in high places... he had no idea! God had provided us with a second miracle. I now wonder how the officer might have reacted if we'd had the time to explain it to him. Instead, we just smiled and thanked him for his efforts as he retreated to the safety of the room behind those glass sliding panels.

Sure enough, another officer soon arrived to lead us through a series of armed security posts and to a full-body metal detector, guarded by a second, armed officer. Tom went through first and immediately set the alarm bells ringing. The armed officer stood to his feet and moved a paper on his desk, allowing us a glimpse of the revolver sitting there, just waiting for one of us to make a wrong move. Our escort quietly asked if Tom was wearing a belt buckle. Lifting his shirt, Tom reached to remove the offending belt, placed it on a plastic tray on the desk then retreated to re-enter the scanner a second time. The car keys were then removed from his pocket and joined the belt on the tray. Through he went a third time, and now there was silence. It was my turn, and I squared up to the beast and stepped through. Again, the alarm bells started to scream.

"Wedding rings," the officer advised. "They will have to come off."

Onto the plastic tray, along with my handbag, as that would not be allowed to go any further. Through I went again. Blessed silence. Now the revolver was covered again, and a small key was handed to Tom.

"Locker 43. You can store your belongings there. They will be safe while you are here, but I will need that key back on your way out." Scary, yes. Intimidating, yes. But we still had a long way to go.

Our personal guard then led us down a long corridor that had several cell blocks leading off to our left. From there, rough voices could be heard yelling out obscenities and verbally threatening each other from behind the relative safety of locked doors. Very afraid now, my heart racing and muscles tightening, I slid my hand into the crook of Tom's arm and instinctively increased my pace. I needed to be away from this area. I don't mind confessing a very real fear in that moment. Those butterflies in my stomach were definitely not flying in formation. I muttered to myself, *Lord, get me out of here, please.*

On to another waiting room and time to relax just a little. Only now did we realise the enormity of the miracle we had just witnessed. Two thousand years ago, God had thrown open a prison door to let Simon Peter *out*. But today, in the Pāremoremo Maximum-Security Unit, the toughest in the country, he had just thrown open several doors to let us *in*.

"Wow... just wow," Tom stuttered, a smile spreading across his handsome face. "We are inside where we should not be allowed. He did that. God really did just do that. Wow!" He reached out and took me into his arms, hugging me tightly, something he hadn't done for a very long time. As he released his hold, all I could think was, Wow, *did he really just do that? Or did God just do that? Either way, Thank you, Lord.*

On now to the parole hearing. We were ushered into a smallish boardroom furnished with two long tables, around which sat eight to ten board members, including a judge. Towards the corner of the room was a much smaller desk where the court stenographer was recording every spoken word. Facing the tables and against one wall were six individual chairs. Daniel sat alone in one of these, his gentle face lighting up as we entered.

The meeting had already started, so for the next few minutes we listened very carefully to what was being said. Board members were reading reports to each other regarding Daniel's record of behaviours and conduct over the last eight years. Someone described him as a 'model inmate', which made me smile. Then we were asked to add any information that might influence the board's decision-making process. Tom was never a man who enjoyed speaking publicly, so gave me a wee nudge and whispered, "Can you do it first, please?" (What, again?)

I stood very still for a second or two, closed my eyes and prayed: "Lord, I am not sure what you need me to say, so I am just going to open my mouth. Please give me your words."

"When we recite the Lord's prayer, we say: 'Forgive us our sins as we forgive those who sin against us.' But how can we expect to receive God's forgiveness unless we are prepared to truly forgive?"

I told something of the love, respect and true friendship we had built over the years of Daniel's incarceration and of our deep desire for his release, sooner rather than later. Christmas was coming up, and our prayer was for Daniel to spend it in the arms of his family, a free man. As I finished speaking, I noticed that several board members had their heads down, fumbling with the papers in front of them.

The judge cleared his throat and thanked me for my contribution. Then, as a box of tissues was passed around the table, he added with a smile, "It is not a good look to leave half the parole board in tears, Mrs Murphy." The Holy Spirit had moved among them with such strength and purpose that day. We were all deeply blessed.

Almost as soon as I sat down, the door opened, and Daniel's parents were escorted into the room. His father, at first, was understandably defensive, asking who we were and what exactly we were doing at this hearing. The judge quickly explained that we were members of the Murphy family and that we had been visiting Daniel for several years and were there now to plead for his son's release, asking the board to allow Daniel to be home with his family in time for Christmas.

Mr D's face flushed deeply. We watched his expression change several times as his mind raced through total confusion, anger, and finally to the sudden realisation of what he had just been told. 'Murphy' was the name of his son's victim, so we had to be family. And if that was true, why were we asking for Daniel's release? Why were we not asking the judge to throw away the key instead? His personal struggle was plain for all to read. Then, at last, we witnessed a huge load being lifted from his shoulders as he finally saw the truth.

This very dear father turned toward Tom and I to ask forgiveness for his rudeness. But instead of a rebuke, he was surprised when my husband stood up and took his hand. "It's OK, mate," Tom said. "We have had a lot of time to get used to this situation. You've only just walked into it."

Mr D turned to his son for the first time in more than eight years and saw a reassuring smile. He then focused his attention on the judge and other board members and found that same reassurance looking back at him. Clearly, he and Mrs D had missed something important, but he couldn't be sure exactly what. There were no angry faces in the room.

The hearing proceeded, and at last, when Daniel's father was invited to speak, he talked of his and Mrs D's pain. He told of Daniel's very strict upbringing as one of six children.

"The word MURDERER is not one that any of us would want to attach to a family member, especially not to one of our own children," he told the board members. He told them of the years filled with anger, shame and disgrace that had prevented him from visiting his son in prison.

My heart ached for all the family days he and Mrs D could and should have shared. For all the opportunities there had been for us to share the gift of forgiveness with them. So many opportunities missed.

*So now faith, hope and love abide, these three;
but the greatest of these is love.*
(1 Corinthians 13:13)

7

Mending Family Ties

Once the hearing had ended, Daniel was allowed to spend a few minutes with his family and ours before being returned to his section. As the five of us gathered, Mrs D stepped forward, wrapped her arms around my neck, buried her face deep in my shoulder and wept, whispering "Thank you," over and over again. Before I knew it, I was weeping, too, as we clung to each other.

A strange and wonderful comfort seemed to envelop us while the men looked on, slightly bewildered by the scene playing out before them. These two ladies, total strangers, weeping together like long-lost sisters. Two mothers experiencing something they could never fully understand or explain except that this was happening just as it needed to be. Something blessed, I think.

A few minutes later, we dried our tears and, arms linked, joined the men in their conversation. Tom and I listened as Daniel's parents caught him up on all the news of his siblings. After eight years of absence, there was a lot to tell. One had married. Another was expecting her third child. A third had moved to a new town with his wife and small family, and on it went. Each sibling's life was given the time and respect they deserved, and Daniel sat, looking slightly bemused as his parents tried to get eight years' worth of news out in as short a time as possible.

It was during this visit that Daniel explained his part in God's miracle. When the guard called the parole hearing room, he advised that members of the Murphy family were at his office wanting to attend the hearing. The judge, who took the call, asked Daniel if he knew anything about us wanting to be there and how he felt about meeting us. Daniel told him he really wanted the Murphys there and that we were his friends. Dear Daniel had no idea God was directing him in that moment.

We were invited to join Mr and Mrs D for lunch in what was then the quaint little Albany shopping precinct before returning home. And what a very special, blessed afternoon that became. Over a simple outdoor lunch of sandwiches and coffee, surrounded by wild chickens that clucked and pecked at the ground around our feet, a bond was forged as we laughed and cried together.

So many memories and stories of Daniel's childhood were shared. Mrs D confided that, of all her children, Daniel was the very last one she had thought of when told by police that her son had been arrested on suspicion of murder. She described a young boy who would carefully carry home lost kittens or baby birds that had fallen out of trees. I sat smiling as I recognised the same gentle characteristics I had come to know so well in our dear friend. With a mother's pride, she spoke of a little boy with a huge heart. Someone who would bring home every waif and stray he could find, both animal and human. Not a murderer. Never that.

Tom and I described in as much detail possible of the incredible road we had travelled with Daniel. We detailed memories of the heartache, tears, laughter, prayers, and a deep loving bond forged as we worked our way out of all that darkness; how we had been aware of God's presence so many times as we moved through the pain to find the joy. Our journey truly exemplified 1 Peter 5:10 (CSB): *And the God of all grace, who called you to his eternal glory in Christ, will himself restore, establish, strengthen and support you after you have suffered a little while.*

And yes, Mrs D and I found ourselves weeping together again as details of so many precious visits were remembered. To lighten the mood a little, I recalled one special family day visit when some of the inmates put together a Pacific Island-themed comedy show for us. To simulate the island drums, a large grass mat was rolled up tightly and the drumsticks were wooden spoons borrowed from the kitchen. These simple tools created an amazing sound to accompany the deep melodic voices as men, some playing the part of women, danced and sang traditional songs. Or at least tried to, between silly jokes and much overacting. Our tears soon turned to laughter as we relayed some of the more outlandish details of the concert.

During that lunch, I discovered that Mrs D was a true lady in every sense of the word. And I learned to admire and respect her gentle nature and wonderful sense of fun. Sadly, she passed away just six months later, without ever seeing her son come home again.

*For I will be merciful toward their iniquities,
and I will remember their sins no more.*
(Hebrews 8:12)

8

A Final Hearing

As is usually the case, Daniel was not granted parole that first time. I was led to understand that prisoners are almost never paroled after a first hearing. It's just the way the system works, I guess.

We all swallowed the disappointment and resumed our usual routine for another year. For Tom and I, our relationship became more comfortable, like a deep friendship built on the years-long journey that had become our life's reality. The halfway house was busier than ever, with some of our young people moving on to be replaced with others who needed our hospitality, friendship and guidance.

Our visits continued as before, and the relationship between Tom and Daniel kept growing. I was often amazed at how comfortable they had become in each other's company and praying together became as natural as breathing.

In October of 1995, we were there again. This time, we ensured all the legal i's were dotted and t's were crossed. The Department of Justice received all the right application forms, and we were granted official permission to attend Daniel's second hearing so that when we arrived at the prison, they would be expecting us.

Again, we were led back to the maximum-security section,

back through the same process as last year, with full-body scans, keys, belts, handbag and wedding rings in the locker, and the same march through long corridors. Only this time we knew what to expect, so it was a little less scary.

We arrived at the hearing room about five minutes early to find Daniel and his dad sitting on a bench seat in the hallway. Both men rose to their feet, and there were handshakes and hugs all around before we settled into quiet conversation. I immediately felt the absence of the missing lady in our group. Daniel's gentle mother was sorely missed that day by everyone, I'm sure.

The hearing was about to start, and Daniel was summoned into the boardroom. Tom, Mr D and I were asked to wait a few minutes as the board members needed to speak with Daniel first. The duty guard assured us that it would take only a short time, and we would all be admitted. Tom and Mr D chatted quietly as we waited. Soon enough, the guard was back, and we followed him into the same board room as last year, and many of the same faces greeted us.

The judge spoke first to Mr D, expressing his condolences on the loss of his wife, before asking if there was anything he wanted the board members to know. This 1995 hearing would be very different for this man than the one he had attended the previous year. This time, he was more comfortable, knowing he was with friends who cared about his son and were as eager to have Daniel home as he was. He spoke quietly, telling of the shift that had taken place in his relationship with his son over the last twelve months and how he was looking forward to having Daniel home again. There was a lot of lost time to make up and he was keen to get started as soon as the board would allow. Being a 'good Kiwi bloke', there were no hearts and flowers in his speech, but he was very clear about the sorrow he felt for the years lost and openly admitted that stubborn male pride had much to do with that.

Soon, we were asked to speak, but politely warned, please, not to leave the board members in tears this time.

Oh dear, during the last twelve months, that judge must have presided over hundreds of parole hearings and heard many, many family impact statements, both positive and negative. But still, he remembered us. More importantly, he remembered what had been said and how God's words had made them all feel.

Today, however, it was Tom who rose to speak, and the stenographer sat poised, ready to record his every word. I saw him glance at her as he cleared his throat. Quietly and calmly, my husband confirmed that everything we needed to say to the board had already been said a year ago and was now a matter of record. That, in the intervening year, nothing had changed. We still cared very deeply for Daniel and were as determined as ever that he should be set free so that he and his family could at last share Christmas together this year. At home, where he belonged.

Tom returned to his seat, and the judge glanced at me as if waiting for me to add something more. I just looked him in the eye, and, without speaking, gave my head a slight shake, confirming there was nothing I could say that Tom had not already said. We were as committed to Daniel's freedom as we had been a year ago. And so, the hearing continued without any further input from the Murphy family.

Long and detailed behavioural reports and evaluations were again presented to the board members, confirming that both the unit manager and prison psychologist were happy that there was no risk to the public or of Daniel reoffending in the future, and they were ready to recommend his release. Our dear friend was even described again as a "model prisoner" by his unit manager, the same manager who had sat watching that touch rugby game years before. A man we had met many times over the years and who knew well the relationship between Daniel and ourselves, the friendship he had often witnessed and now remarked on.

Almost exactly one month later, we received another collect call from the prison. And again, an excited Daniel was on the line, giggling like a child who had just discovered that all his Christmases had come at once. The parole board decision had come through. He was to be released into the care of his family in just three weeks!

Who could have known that three short weeks would take so long to pass? We were all so excited that we thought the day would never come. Our dear friend was going home at last.

After speaking with his dad, Daniel asked if we would like to collect him from the prison on release day and drive him to his South Auckland home, where a pot-luck lunch would be shared with all his siblings and their families. "The Murphys are responsible for dessert," he laughed.

In the last few months leading up to his second parole hearing, Tom and I had started putting a little money away each week. We knew this day would arrive eventually, and we wanted to be well-prepared for it. No surprises this year. Since Alex and James were to come with us this time, letters were written to each of their teachers, stating our intention to take them out of school that day, that the family would be traveling to Auckland on important business.

When James presented his letter to the school, his teacher

read it carefully and then asked James what was happening in Auckland. Was it to be a special occasion, and was he excited to go? The truth was told openly. James simply said that we were going to see the "man who murdered Grandad". We were going to take him home from prison, so yes, it was going to be a very special day. Astonished, the teacher asked why. Why in the world would we do that? Why would the family support the release of a murderer?

Without hesitation, James said: "Because we love him". I believe the teacher was left speechless. Such simple wisdom out of the mouth of a child. I could not have expressed it better myself.

Praise the Lord, O my soul!
(Psalm 146:1)

9

Freedom at Last

At last, the big day arrived, and early in the morning, pavlova, trifle and fresh fruit salad were carefully packed into chilly bins (coolers) and stacked in the boot of the car. I figured we could pick up ice cream and cream once we got to Auckland, no sense in it melting in the car. The forecast had been for sunshine and blue skies all day, and the forecasters had pegged it right. What a beautiful summer morning. It felt like God was smiling as we bundled the now-teenaged boys into the car and set out on the road. Taking the Auckland freeway morning rush hour into account, the trip would take about ninety minutes, so we left early.

Crossing the Waihou River on the old Kopu bridge, I sat watching the sunshine winking off the water flowing far below us, like tiny stars in a bright blue sky, trees and shrubs along the riverbank swaying in the gentle breeze.

Passing through farmland bathed in the summer warmth and small settlements along the way, Pipiroa, Waitakaruru, Maramarua, Mangatāwhiri and on to Pōkeno, where we would enter the Southern Freeway, all we had to do now was to follow the road all the way to Albany, then on to Pāremoremo and Daniel. All seemed right in our world today.

The closer we got to the prison, the better the day was getting. Excitement was building in the backseat as Alex and James talked of the upcoming visit to the 'D' household, wondering how many others would be there and what might be for lunch. Tom was smiling and happy. I knew he had been looking forward to this day for a long time. All the years of visiting and waiting were over at last, and we had been given the privilege of driving Daniel home. How I wished Mrs D could have been there to enjoy this day with us. I knew how proud and happy she would have been. I would miss her hugs today.

At precisely 10 am, our family pulled up outside the minimum-security unit and parked the car. All of us were excited as we presented ourselves to the officer at the outside gate. Daniel was already standing on the far side inside the double-gated exit, chatting with a second officer. We stood on the outside, my sons smiling and waving as Daniel was ushered through the first gate and watched as that gate closed behind him. Then, after a few seconds, the outside gate shuddered and squeaked. Too slowly it began moving, inching its way across the opening, until there was finally enough room for him to step through. We all had to stand still and wait for that outer gate to completely close, but the moment it clanged shut, Alex and James stepped forward.

Poor Daniel had to drop his bags to avoid being bowled over. Hugs and laughter followed before Tom and I could even get close enough to greet him. I knew how the boys felt about Daniel but wondered if they realised this was the last time they would ever be at Pāremoremo again. From today, Daniel was free to catch up with us anywhere and at any time he wanted. He was truly free at last. Hallelujah!

Squeezing into the back seat between two wriggling teens, Daniel sat with an arm around each of them, listening to all their many questions and answering each in turn as best he could, now and then calling directions to the front seat.

"This man is not going to get a single moment to himself today if we don't corral those boys," I whispered to Tom.

"Let's just hope there are lots of young people at the house to distract them for a while," he replied as he took the off-ramp.

Pulling into the driveway a few minutes later, we were met with a sea of faces; five siblings with five spouses and about a dozen children of varying ages, all smiling and waving. And there, front and centre, Mr D, his hands hung loosely at his sides, staring at the spot where his son still sat. Even from the car, I could see he was fighting to control his emotions.

"OK boys, you need to let Daniel out," Tom said. "He's been waiting a long time for today. Don't hold the man up now."

Alex was the first out. "Open the boot, Tom," he called as he headed toward the rear of the car. Soon, he and James had the bags and chilly bins out as eager hands reached to help carry them inside. Mr D stepped forward as Daniel emerged from the car. Arms wide open, he embraced his son tightly, turning him toward the front door. Brothers and sisters slapped their prodigal brother on the back in familial greeting.

One sister greeted us and led the way through the front door, where more friends and family awaited Daniel's arrival with eager anticipation. Suddenly, noise and laughter were everywhere. Everyone wanted Daniel's attention. And very soon, we knew he needed to be rescued.

Tom nudged one of the many brothers, pointing in Daniel's direction. "I think he might need some air, mate," he whispered.

With all the subtlety that South Auckland is known for (not), Daniel was quickly extracted by his brothers and ushered out the back door. There, alone with his siblings for the first time in almost a decade, Daniel finally began to relax. Someone handed him a drink and pointed him down the garden where 'the boys' of the family could surround and protect him.

Inside, the kitchen began to fill as final preparations got underway for the lunch. And now I remembered we hadn't stopped for the cream and ice cream. You just can't have trifle without cream. And fruit salad is nothing without ice cream on top.

"Is there a dairy close by?" I asked. "Sure. There's one just around the corner. Daniel knows the way. He might want to go for a walk about now."

One of the youngsters was sent to find Uncle Daniel and bring him to the kitchen. "Can you walk Miriam to the dairy please, bro? She needs to get ice cream."

"Cool. Let's go." Daniel was sounding a little too keen to go, I thought. This day had turned out to be more intense than he had anticipated. The need for ice cream was the perfect excuse to get him away from all the excitement. For the first few minutes of our walk, Daniel said nothing as he guided me down the road, turning right into a narrow alleyway leading to a local school's back field.

"Shortcut," he said as we began the long trek across the grass. At about the halfway point, he suddenly stopped dead in his tracks, and as I came up beside him, I was unceremoniously picked up and whirled around several times in his arms. Great peals of laughter came from this man who had been so quiet a moment before. "I'm free!" he shouted. "I'm free! I can go wherever I please. And I'm never going back there again." As he gently placed me back on solid ground, his step became lighter, and he was smiling brightly as we made our way between classrooms, out the front gate and on to the dairy.

Now, for the first time, he understood what today was all about. Now he remembered freedom in a way he never had before. Now it was precious, an amazing blessing to be savoured and something he would never take for granted again. We both smiled all the way home, knowing that our moment on the rugby field would not be mentioned to anyone. He smiled because he finally understood the true meaning of the freedom he had been given. I smiled because my very dear friend had his life back at last.

The last nine years were done now. Our loving heavenly Father had taken us all through the valley of the shadow of death and had led us out the other side. Forgiven, healed, restored, and strengthened, Daniel was supported by a large family who loved him dearly and would be there for him as he navigated his way through this new life in a place that had changed so much over the years.

Daniel had sinned greatly. He had suffered greatly as a result. He had learned that our heavenly Father is not an angry, vengeful God, but a loving faithful Saviour who met him in his darkest hours, ready and willing to forgive and build him up again. A God who loves to love and be loved.

The last time I spoke with Daniel was in the early 2000s. He was happy and settled, with a wonderful lady who knows his full story and loves him anyway. He is retired now and loves spending time with his family. I don't feel he would want the world to know anything more than that.

*It was fitting to celebrate and be glad,
for this your brother was dead, and is alive;
he was lost, and is found.*
(Luke 15:32)

*Then my soul will rejoice in the Lord,
exulting in His salvation.*
(Psalm 35:9)

10

It Takes a Lot of Love to Forgive

Learning to truly repent and accept forgiveness, not just from his victim's family but from the God who made him, was not an easy journey for Daniel. His profound sense of guilt hung like a stone around his neck for too many years. Satan had him convinced he was worthless, written off, completely without hope, so why even try? But our gentle master, Jesus Christ, had other ideas. He went willingly to the cross to save *all* sinners. Not just the ones who have sinned a little bit

In Luke 23:40-43 (NIV), the thief who hung on the cross next to Jesus rebuked his fellow criminal for mocking Jesus, saying:

"Don't you fear God," the first thief said, "since you are under the same sentence? We are punished justly, for we are getting what our deeds deserve. But this man has done nothing wrong." Then he said, "Jesus, remember me when you come into your kingdom."

Jesus answered him, "Truly I tell you, today you will be with me in paradise."

With His dying breaths coming in great agonising gasps, Jesus still showed compassion and mercy for a 'hopeless' sinner. He, even in His agony, was ready and willing to forgive a repentant heart.

Daniel, too, had been forgiven, but he needed to learn how to receive that grace and forgiveness. He had to forgive himself for his past. It would take time to accept that so much love even exists, and that our Lord had known Daniel and had a plan for his life, even as he was being formed in his mother's womb. That he was loved and cherished unconditionally by the Father who created him.

Hebrews 8:12 (NIV) says: *For I will forgive their wickedness and will remember their sins no more.* Again, in Hebrews 10:16-17 (NIV), we read: *This is the covenant I will make with them after that time, says the Lord. I will put my laws in their hearts, and I will write them on their minds.* Then he adds: *Their sins and lawless acts I will remember no more.*

These verses spoke to Tom and I as we began to build our very personal relationship with Willard's killer. We could so easily have allowed ourselves to continue wallowing in self-righteous anger and bitterness. We had to learn that same true forgiveness and move forward as if that sin had never happened. I give you fair warning. That process takes a lot of love and is not for the faint-hearted. But remember, the Word tells us: *With man this is impossible, but with God all things are possible* (Matthew 19:26 NIV). We had to learn to trust God completely and let all self-righteousness go.

Colossians 3:13-14 is another passage which speaks of our responsibility to forgive: *...bearing with one another and forgiving one another if anyone has a grievance against another. Just as the Lord has forgiven you, so you are also to forgive. Above all, put on love, which is the perfect bond of unity.* (CSB)

We must give the situation to Jesus. Wow, it sounds so easy, but it is not easy at all. We have an inbuilt need to take control and direct our own lives. But this is not God's nature. We had to get on our knees so many times to ask for His strength to get us through. If you think for one moment that you can do this alone, let me tell you, you are kidding yourself. And the enemy will eat you up and spit you out before he's even had breakfast. I will say it again. This process is not for the faint-hearted, so don't try it without wearing the full armour of God.

How do we dress ourselves in the six pieces of armour God has given us to fight and be victorious in spiritual warfare (Ephesians 6:11-18)?

I think this was best described by Tony Evans, Senior Pastor of Oak Cliff Bible Fellowship in Dallas, Texas, when he said: "The answer is prayer."

Put on the belt of truth by declaring to God that you believe what He says.

Put on the breastplate of righteousness by acting based on God's Word, wanting to please Him in all you do.

Put on the sandals of the gospel of peace when you say, "God confirmed this situation", or "He has caused me discomfort, so I shouldn't move ahead with my plans."

Put on the shield of faith by acting in the knowledge that God's Word is truth and asking Him to support you in your actions.

Put on the helmet of salvation in prayer when you ask God to clear your mind of anything that would distract you from operating within His will.

Put on the sword of the Spirit when you quote Scripture and ask God to show you the right Scriptures to use.

Prayer has been described as the first form of email; God's way of communicating with you, especially when you are under attack, so the devil has no option but to flee from you.

So, go to Him first. Get on your knees and ask for *His presence and strength* to get you through.

If you really want this, if you really, really want it, Our Lord and Saviour will step up beside you. He will strengthen you. He will hold you when you hurt. He will comfort you and heal your shattered heart. And He will bless you beyond measure.

He will walk through the flood with you every step of the way.

And remember, expect to be blessed with His mercy, grace and freedom from the pain. True forgiveness draws you into the very heart of God.

Dear reader, your life can change in the blink of an eye. Everything that is firm and unshakable in your life can be ripped away in a moment.

But if there is just one thing left for you to cling to, make it Jesus. Trust in the love He has for you. Trust that, no matter what happens, He will share it with you. When you learn to keep your eyes above the storm and focus solely on Him, He is there, lovingly, wholly dependable and infinitely trustworthy. He loves you. He sees you. And He stands waiting, always ready to forgive and heal a repentant heart.

For you have been called to live in freedom,
my brothers and sisters.
But don't use your freedom to satisfy your sinful nature.
Instead, use your freedom to serve one another in love.
(Galatians 5:13 TLB)

PART TWO

The Hard Bits

11

The Cracks Start to Show

I admit that these next chapters have absolutely been the hardest to write – so much so that I almost didn't. However, I promised I would tell it all (even the hard bits), and a promise made, must be kept. Here is where God's call for brutal honesty and spiritual transparency gets incredibly difficult.

Some time ago, I asked the Lord what lesson he wanted to convey to you from this section of the book, and to my surprise, there are two lessons – the importance of forgiveness, yes, of course. And I think we've covered that. But the second lesson was about Tom, about me, and about exercising absolute trust in our Saviour when our world was falling apart around our feet. It's about two imperfect people whose hearts were so dreadfully broken by some of the worst events of the past decade, and whose lives had been ripped apart spiritually and physically by their own hands.

While we were concentrating on Daniel, we both neglected our own walks with Jesus and managed to, somehow, leave Him out of our own, very personal hurts. Two dearly loved children of God who each took their own pain into the wilderness. Each of us built towers around our hearts with walls so high and stone fortifications so thick and so seemingly unbreakable that we could no longer see God's heart, hear His voice, or even experience his presence in our lives. Those walls were built with our pain, self-righteous anger, pride, betrayal, and self-protection against the world and everyone in it.

But they also locked out a life more abundant – walls that would soon shut out everything that we loved, including our marriage, our fellowship with God, and with some members of our own families.

The destroyer found the smallest cracks in our spirits and sent his minions to rip those cracks wide open. In our grief and confusion, we, each in our own way, allowed it to happen.

* * *

Christmas was coming up, and Tom and I had been given a month's leave. A house truck was provided by friends, and money donated for petrol and provisions. The plan was to take the first few days to travel to Cape Reinga (Te Rerenga Wairua), the most northern tip of New Zealand. Neither of us had ever been that far north and really wanted to see it. Wikipedia states that for Māori, Cape Reinga is the most spiritually significant place in New Zealand. An ancient pōhutukawa tree and a lonely lighthouse mark this special place. After death, all Māori spirits are said to travel up the coast and over the wind-swept vista to the pōhutukawa tree on the headland of Te Rerenga Wairua. It is also where the Pacific Ocean meets the Tasman Sea, creating a spectacular line of waves reaching as far as the eye can see.

We would spend a couple of days there before making our way down the upper east coast of the North Island to Tauranga in the Bay of Plenty, then on down to East Cape in time for Christmas, just a week away.

Last year's Christmas break had not been so extensive and

was spent in the quiet of an 'off the grid' country cottage owned by friends who would be away for an extended break themselves. This year, I was looking forward to an adventure and was excited to go when and where we pleased for a whole month. After a particularly busy year for Te Whare Manaaki, we both needed time alone to recover, regroup and try and mend the years-long rift in our marriage. As I packed, emotions blended with fragments of precious memories, and I imagined myself lying quietly in Tom's arms again. This time away from the world would help us mend, I was sure of it.

Tom remained quietly withdrawn during those first few days, becoming more animated only when we sat playing card games in the evenings or sharing the cooking duties in the very compact kitchen area. Once we left the Cape and started the southward journey, our days became lighter as we explored new places and shared new adventures together. It was good to see him begin to relax and enjoy the trip.

That month went by in a blur of new sights and sounds, lazy days and warm summer evenings spent enjoying each other's company. However, I was always aware of something I could not name or even truly identify. Although Tom had seemed to enjoy our time alone together, this *something* was standing between us. And now, all intimacy was gone. No words were ever spoken about it. No discussion or decisions made. Just gone. The scary thing was that Tom, still a young man at 45, didn't seem to mind a bit. I wanted our marriage back, all of it. But how in the world could that happen if only one of us was invested in it?

As much as I craved it, I could not hear God's voice in the darkness and could not admit, even to myself, that I could not hear Him while my heart was in self-protection mode.

Tom and I now had friendship, companionship, precious

shared memories, but not a marriage. The last decade had left indelible marks on us. The marks were entirely unique. We had both witnessed and survived the same things and were very far from the two people who had started this journey in 1986. But if there was a way forward from this point, we would have to fight for it. And as we made our way back to Te Whare Manaaki at the end of our leave, I determined to do just that.

In your righteousness, rescue me and deliver me...
(Psalm 71:2 NIV)

12

Betrayal

As Tom pulled the house truck into the driveway, several of our young people poured out the front door to greet us, along with the lovely couple, Brian and Julie, who had been looking after them in our absence. It was good to be home again.

Many hands helped us unpack and clean the truck before we could return it to its owners. I followed the truck with our van, then drove Tom home again. There would be an evening meal to prepare before this day was done. However, Brian and Julie were gone when we returned, and as we entered the house, we found our pastor, John, sitting in the dining room, waiting to speak with us... about Ruby.

Ruby had been with us at Te Whare Manaaki for a little under a year when she decided she wanted a small apartment of her own. She had become very close to her 'surrogate dad' Tom and I during our time together, so I was happy that she felt ready to step out of her 'safe' place, knowing that we would always be there for her. She found a tiny, one-bedroom flat in the centre of town and had great fun setting up her first home and creating a cosy nest for herself.

However, John's news was devastating. Ruby was in hospital in a mental health unit. Hiding, it seemed. During our time away, she confessed to John that she and Tom had been lovers for the last ten months. Then, as our return home drew nearer, she grew more and more afraid of what Tom might have said to me. John explained that all my possible reactions had panicked her, so she had packed up, left her new home and admitted herself to the hospital. As he spoke, it was plain that John struggled to remain calm. And as he left, I saw him glance at Tom, a look of real anger and disappointment in his eyes.

In that moment, my whole world collapsed around me. This could not be true! Tom and I trusted each other. He would not do this to me. Could Ruby have been mistaken or could John have misunderstood? Please God, this cannot be true.

With tear-filled eyes barely able to focus, I asked two of the older girls to start dinner and then turned to my husband.

"We need to talk. Now," I whispered. And with that, I picked up the keys and headed out to the van, climbed into the passenger seat, and waited. Tom soon joined me, reached for the keys, backed the van into the street, and turned toward the centre of town. We had gone less than half a kilometre when he pulled the van onto a grassed area and killed the engine.

At first, the silence was deafening, and then suddenly, the lights went on in my soul. Like a wrecking ball, the truth of the last decade came crashing in on me. For the first time I saw that Tom had only ever considered his own pain. Never once had the pain of others entered his mind.

"How long, Tom? How many times? When were you going to tell me? Was it ever in our home? In our bed?"

Tears welled up in his eyes as Tom finally let it all out. It was true. All of it. And yes, several times it had happened in our home. In our bed. Ruby had once even left Tom to make the bed as she came out to help with meal preparation and called me Aunty Mum.

The totality of treachery and betrayal was devastating. I needed to escape this nightmare, so jumped out of the van and ran. It had started to rain, but still I ran. As fast as I could, I ran. Soaked to the skin, I just had to keep moving.

Sometime later, I found myself clear across town. Just ahead of me was a supermarket, so I went in and asked to use the phone. I made a call to the only friend I could think of who would care without comment and support without asking questions.

Through my tears, I explained where to find me, then staggered outside and sat in the pouring rain, weeping bitterly. Now, all the old grief was crashing in around me again. Just a few hours ago, I had been so positive, so ready to fight for my marriage. But how could I fight this? I had trusted Tom with my whole life. I loved him so much that I couldn't imagine a day without him being in it. After all we had been through together, how could this have happened? Now, at least, I understood the *something* and what had changed in our marriage, though it brought me no comfort, only more questions. How did I not see this? Did my love and trust blind me to what was happening right under my nose? How could I have been so mistaken?

Wet, cold and tired, I was dropped back to the house some hours later to be met by a very angry James demanding to know where I had been and why I was in such a state. Tom sat at the dining table with his head down, not daring to look at me. Te Whare Manaaki was no place to keep secrets, so they all knew something bad had happened even before my return. First though, I needed a hot shower and dry clothes, then a conversation needed to be had.

That conversation lasted well into the night. Sometimes loud and angry. Sometimes quiet and filled with sorrow. But as a new day dawned, I was alone in my grief. Tom had packed what he could carry and left Te Whare Manaaki.

There were going to be a million questions. Alex and James would want to know where Tom had gone and why. Why were so many of his belongings gone? Where would he live now? And who was going to help me manage Te Whare Manaaki?

Then, there would be the inevitable questions asked by bewildered residents. Tom had not only broken my trust, but the children's and resident's. How could this feel like a safe place for them now? And how in the world would I explain this to the house trustees?

Turn your ear to me, come quickly to my rescue;
be my rock of refuge, a strong fortress to save me.
(Psalm 31:2 NIV)

Make haste to help me, O Lord, my salvation.
(Psalm 38:22)

13

An Ending

I received a call the next day from Pastor John, asking if he and his wife could visit.

"Sure," I said. "But can you give me an hour to let all our people eat and leave the house, please? They all know something is very wrong. I don't think we need to involve them any further just yet."

As everyone trickled into the dining room for breakfast, I knew I owed them some sort of explanation, but the words would not come.

James was the first to speak. "Is he gone? The dining room door is glass, Mum. We all heard you both in here last night."

Soon, others joined in with comments and questions like "Are you leaving too?" and "Will the house close?" Everyone was talking at once, and I couldn't keep up.

"Stop! Please give me a moment to breathe. I will answer all your questions, one at a time."

Over breakfast, I tried to reassure everyone that the house trustees would need to make decisions about the home's future, but at least in the meantime, nothing would change. Yes, Tom had gone (I didn't know where yet), but I was still going to be there. I was still their Auntie Mum, and I would be there for them for as long as I was able.

During the pastor's visit, I was advised of two decisions that had already been made. Firstly, Tom would need to find somewhere else to live as the church leaders did not feel it was morally right for him to remain at the halfway house.

Heartbreakingly, after the revelations of the past 24 hours, I understood this decision completely. The safety and well-being of our young men and women was paramount. To put their minds at ease, I briefly explained that Tom had already left the house and assured John his wishes would be respected. Tom would no longer be a house parent at Te Whare Manaaki.

Secondly, a special deacons' meeting had been called for the following week to try to work out what disciplinary actions, if any, should be taken regarding his indiscretions. As a deacon, I had no option but to be there. Lord, help me! Already decisions were being made that would affect my future and Tom's, even though neither of us had the slightest idea of what to do or even what we wanted.

Once they left, I called Tom's cell phone and was grateful he answered.

"Tom," I said, "I have just had a visit from John. There are some things you and I need to talk about. Can we meet here this afternoon, please?"

At 2:00 pm, I was sitting at the kitchen table with a half-cold coffee in my hand, my mind a million miles away. What would I say to my husband? Would he even come? And if he did arrive, would he want to hear what I had to say? Would he even listen?

I was so distracted by my thoughts that I didn't even notice Tom's arrival until he was making himself comfortable in the seat across from mine.

Over the next 20 minutes, we spoke quietly, each trying to be respectful of the other. Each trying so hard to be polite in the most impolite moment we'd ever shared. And as Tom rose to leave, I placed my hand on his shoulder and quietly said, "I forgive you... Please leave that house key on the table before you go." In the years after Willard's death, I had learned that forgiveness was the only way. It is what brought us safely through those years. So, even on one of the darkest days of my life, I had to make myself say the words and mean them.

However, depression very quickly settled on my spirit. The enemy was pushing me down to a place I had never been before. I lived and breathed for my husband, and now it felt like he was being ripped away from me by others. This was *our* marriage. How can someone else manage that? The destroyer is more than happy to whisper hurtful lies into an already broken heart. I was so shell-shocked that I was finding it hard to even comprehend what I was being asked to deal with.

> *He dragged me from the path and mangled me*
> *and left me without help.*
> (Lamentations 3:11 NIV)

An understanding couple from our congregation offered Tom a room in their home, and the deacons' meeting was set for the following Thursday. In the meantime, I did everything I could to keep Te Whare Manaaki running by myself. Already, one or two of our more troublesome young men had decided that a woman alone could be easily 'managed', but quickly realised that was a mistake. In those first few days, God gave me the strength to deal with the residents, but privately, I was falling apart, and I knew it. One afternoon, I was visited by the pastor's wife, who, while trying to be compassionate and caring, suggested that my mood around the home could be improved just a little. As tears welled up yet again, an unrighteous anger rose up from the very depths of me and burst out unbidden.

"How can you tell me the 'right' way to behave in this situation? You could only know the 'right way' when you have stood where I am standing. But you and I both know, here is a place you will never find yourself. John would never betray you. Never live a lie with you. Do not tell me what you cannot know!" (Lord, forgive me.)

This dear lady simply responded by gently wrapping me in her arms and held me without speaking as I wept bitterly for what seemed like hours.

* * *

On Thursday evening, before leaving the house, I had picked up a small, fist-sized stone and placed it in my coat pocket without knowing why. And as I walked into the parish meeting room, all the other deacons were there. Their conversation quickly died as I entered the room. Tom arrived a short time later and the meeting got underway.

Within only a few minutes, I had the very real feeling that decisions had already been made and that they were here only to pronounce the verdict and sentencing. People started using words like 'sanctions' and 'penalty' and 'removal from current position' and 'forbidden to partake of communion'. But the current state of our marriage or the notion of forgiveness wasn't raised at all.

At some point, I decided enough was enough and found myself on my feet.

"Excuse me," I started. "I think this has gone on quite long enough. Firstly, this man is my husband, and I have forgiven him. Secondly, I always thought that communion was created by Jesus in remembrance of the price He paid for our sins. Surely that cannot be denied to a repentant sinner." Then, reaching into my pocket, I pulled out the stone and carefully placed it on the table. "Let the one without sin be the first to pick it up."

Right here, I openly confess that I overreacted. I was still trying to process Tom's betrayal, to me, to Ruby, and to the ministry we had taken on together. And in that moment, I was finding it almost impossible to grasp that I was also losing my marriage.

For a second or two, there was total silence. Then I stood, carefully placed my chair back in its place and glanced at Tom, who rose, pushed his chair in and followed me out the door. Neither of us said a word as we made our way, each to our own homes, both instinctively knowing it was over. Though it would take some time, I had to accept that sometimes it's OK to genuinely forgive and respectfully walk away. One day, my heart would truly accept that. But not today. Today, the pain was too hard. Too big.

I am reminded of a conversation I had with my mother just after we had accepted the halfway house ministry. I remember telling her that I had the very real feeling that one of us would not survive the task ahead of us. I could never have imagined that it would be our marriage that would die.

* * *

There was still something for me to do. I had to visit Ruby, hug her, and tell her she was forgiven. If I could forgive murder, this simple act should have been a lot easier than it was. But unlike Willard, Tom and Ruby had not died. They were still very much alive. Even after all the lies and betrayal, and as hard as I tried, I couldn't get Tom out of my heart. But nor could I just turn my back on Ruby without releasing the pain and forgiving her.

So now, as I pushed down an unholy need for 'justice', I went to the hospital. There was another conversation that needed to be had. Ruby was not in her room, so I sat on the end of her bed and waited while asking God, "Father, you gave me Your words once before; please give them to me again. I need You here with me as I do this."

When Ruby walked into her room and saw me there, she looked horrified, like a ghost was sitting on her bed. I was the last person she wanted to see. I went to her, held her tightly, and whispered, "I forgive you."

We sat together for a few minutes, speaking of things I cannot repeat before I hugged her again and left. I was not as relieved as I thought I would be. Not yet, at least. This one would take time.

And just as I had done in 1986, I attended to business, so I wouldn't have to think, or feel. Within a month I had resigned my positions as a deacon and in the church office, passed the home management of Te Whare Manaaki over to new house parents, bade my young residents a tearful farewell, and moved into a rural cottage. In all reality, the halfway house needed to be managed by a strong, committed couple, not a now-single woman in the depths of depression, struggling desperately to keep her sanity. And with two teenaged sons, who bravely faced the end of their mother's marriage but had no real understanding of all that had taken place.

By 1998, as divorce proceedings started, I began to understand for the first time what might make a person decide that ending their life was the only way out. Although I never considered it for myself, I was learning to understand it.

An Ending

The last conversation I had with Tom was not pleasant. At last, I understood how the enemy had completely blinded my husband to the true seriousness of his actions. There was no sense of regret evident in his demeanour. There was no understanding of the consequences of what he had done. He just knew he had lost both a wife and a lover. And somehow, that was my fault. The last words I heard from his mouth were: "This just goes to show that our entire marriage has been a complete waste of my time." (May the Lord forgive and be merciful to him.) This left me speechless.

Now, the crushing grief completely overwhelmed me, and I just wanted to run again, to get as far from the pain as fast as I could. Only Jesus could pull me out of the darkness I was living in. But first, I had to ask Him to help me, and I was not ready to do that. This time, I was running from God, Himself, and I would not be ready to talk to Him again for more than 20 years.

But what can I say?
He has spoken to me, and he himself has done this.
I will walk humbly all my years
because of this anguish of my soul.
(Isaiah 38:15 NIV)

14

He Never Left Me

I felt the overwhelming urge to leave New Zealand. I needed to be someplace where nobody knew me or the pain I was living with. I needed time to heal and to find *me* again.

I spoke with my boys, now young men and discussed my need to leave New Zealand. I had cousins in Melbourne and decided that was the place I wanted to be. Each of my sons was invited to come with me.

"Let's all go together," I suggested. "Let's start a new life together where nobody knows us." But Alex and James were adults now, each with their own job and home. Each seeing lovely young ladies they had no intention of leaving behind.

So, in January of 2000, I boarded a plane and flew to Melbourne, where I was met by a cousin who allowed me to stay in his home while I got my feet back on the ground and found a job.

I remember the day I took the train down to Dandenong, where I visited the Australian Tax Department to have a tax number issued. After my appointment, I wandered over to the Dandenong Plaza and bought a cup of coffee at an outdoor cafe. As I enjoyed the sunshine, I observed hundreds of people coming and going all around me and for some strange reason, it filled me with gratitude. I did not recognise a single face. I was totally anonymous in that place. It gave me the first sense of freedom I had felt for a very long time.

Living and working in Melbourne afforded me the delusion that life could be better, somehow. A belief that a new life, new job, and new country could turn my world around and give me peace again. But now, all these years later, I know I could not have been more wrong.

Although I didn't recognise it at the time, there was a huge, Jesus-shaped hole in my heart. I remember once telling my sister that God was done with me. I really believed that whatever He wanted me to do was done. And if my life came to an end now, I was OK with that. (I can almost hear Him laughing at me now.) Looking back, I understand that even when I refused to look at Him, Jesus stood beside me every minute of every day of every year that I was away.

In October 2004, I returned to New Zealand and soon took up employment in a government agency in the Manawatū, where I lived and worked for more than 16 years. (Side note: In 2015, I discovered that Tom had remarried. For reasons I cannot even explain today, I was devastated. Now he truly was completely out of my reach.)

In 2022, retired now and a great grandmother, I moved to the Tararua to be closer to the people I loved the most. Over twenty years after breaking off contact with the Lord, I was still unwilling to speak with Him. There, in my new home, I hibernated from the world for about six months, contenting myself with the house and garden. Again, I found myself in a place where nobody knew me, and it gave me a new sense of peace and rest that I had not felt for many years. It was while in that new home the Lord nudged me once again as if to ask, *"Are you ready now, child?"* The Shepherd had left the 99 and come looking for me.

And yes, now I was ready to finally lay down the old, self-defensive me. Break down all those fortifications and return to the fold. Even today, I'm not entirely sure if that was my idea or His. But I will be forever grateful for it.

At last, I was ready to confess, repent, and be obedient to my Lord. However, that meant finding a fellowship and committing to attend church regularly. To my shame, my reaction to this idea was, "Oh well... Alright then... If I must." You see, it had taken me so long to turn and look at Him again. I was embarrassed that, all those years ago, I had not trusted God enough, not leaned on Him enough, not allowed Him to carry me when I could not walk with Him.

But even though I felt this way, God honoured my recommitment to him by planting me in a fellowship filled with Jesus-loving men and women who made me feel welcomed and accepted right from the first day. These wonderful people have adopted, supported, and loved me as one of their own.

Since coming back to God, like the return of the prodigal daughter, He has blessed me time and time again, emotionally, physically, spiritually, and financially. There has never been a need that He has not met. Day after day, my Father shows His love for me in the smallest things, like the glory of a sunrise, or the sound of birdsong in the early morning. And in the way He links together seemingly unrelated situations to bring about His purpose for my life. It is usually only after these events have taken place that I look back and connect the dots, causing me to look up, smile, and say, "I just know that was you". And, after all these years, I have finally been obedient to His call and written my story down.

***

My prayer is that someone will read this testimony and recognise their own struggle between these pages, that the words God has given me will speak to a lost heart and give someone the strength to seek and find forgiveness, healing, and redemption.

Remember Romans 8:28 (CSB): *We know that all things work together for the good of those who love God, who are called according to His purpose.*

Paul says, "*all things*"... Not just the good and happy moments of our lives but the hard, sad and painful ones, too. All moments can show God's glory and goodness. Though it might sometimes seem hard to believe, God works *everything* together for the good of those who love Him. This doesn't mean that everything will seem good in the moment, or that everything will work out the way we hope it will. After all, we live in a broken, messy world. But we can cling to the sure knowledge that the Holy Spirit is at work in our lives every day, interceding, advocating, celebrating and grieving right alongside us.

As we read further, Romans 8:35 (CSB) says: *Who can separate us from the love of Christ? Can affliction, or distress, or persecution, or famine, or nakedness, or danger, or sword?*

When life's battles get too much for us to bear, there's only one place left to go. We must go before our heavenly Father with all our pain, brokenness, fear and damage. We must beg Him for the spiritual tools we will need to break down those self-made fortifications in our hearts.

God loves us so much that he has already given us those tools (His Word, His grace, love, peace, and eternal promises), but only we can wield those tools. As described in this book, forgiveness is an essential key God asks us to use.

When we recite the Lord's prayer, we say, *Forgive us our sins as we forgive those who sin against us.* But how can we expect to receive God's forgiveness unless we, ourselves, are prepared to truly forgive?

I believe there are people in this world, dedicated Christians, who have been given the tools of God, and I want to speak directly to you. I don't know who you are, where you live, or even if you are male or female, but please believe that God has heard your cries and has felt your pain. He has sat with you as you've wept and has given you the tools you need, but unforgiveness, pride, resentment, pain, and misguided self-reliance refuses to allow you to unpack them. Please don't spend another unnecessary day in the wilderness.

Look for the One who created you. The One who has loved you since before the world was formed. The One who has promised never to leave your side for a single moment. Seek His face. Seek His heart, and you will find Him. Listen for His voice and trust in His love for you, even in the midst of the greatest storm you will ever face.

Amen

Helpful Scriptures for Further Study

But with you there is forgiveness, that you may be feared.
(Psalm 130:4)

To the Lord our God belong mercy and forgiveness,
for we have rebelled against Him.
(Daniel 9:9)

For if you forgive other people when they sin against you,
your heavenly Father will also forgive you.
But if you do not forgive others their sins,
your Father will not forgive your sins.
(Matthew 6:14-15 NIV)

Then Peter came up and said to Him,
"Lord, how often will my brother sin against me,
and I forgive him? As many as seven times?"
Jesus said to him, "I do not say to you seven times,
but seventy-seven times."
(Matthew 18:21-22)

Jesus looked at them and said, "With man this is impossible,
but with God all things are possible."
(Matthew 19:26 NIV)

And whenever you stand praying, forgive,
if you have anything against anyone, so that your Father
who is in heaven may forgive you your sins.
(Mark 11:25)

And Jesus said, "Father, forgive them, for they know not
what they do." And they cast lots to divide his garments.
(Luke 23:34)

If we confess our sins, He is faithful and just to forgive us our
sins and to cleanse us from all unrighteousness.
(John 1:9)

If you forgive the sins of any, they are forgiven.
If you withhold forgiveness from any, it is withheld.
(John 20:23)

Let it be known to you therefore, brothers,
that through this man forgiveness of sins
is proclaimed to you.
(Acts 13:38)

God exalted him at his right hand as leader and saviour,
to give repentance to Israel and forgiveness of sins...
(Acts 5:31)

Therefore, as God's chosen ones, holy and dearly loved,
put on compassion, kindness, humanity, gentleness,
and patience, bearing with one another and forgiving one
another if anyone has a grievance against another.
Just as the Lord has forgiven you, so you are also to forgive.

Above all, put on love, which is the perfect bond of unity.
And let the peace of Christ, to which you are also called
in the body, rule your hearts. And be thankful.
(Colossians 3:12-15 CSB)

In Him we have redemption through His blood,
the forgiveness of our trespasses to the riches of His grace.
(Ephesians 1:71)

Be kind to one another, tenderhearted, forgiving one another,
as God in Christ forgave you.
(Ephesians 4:32)

God exalted him at his right hand as Leader and Saviour,
to give repentance to Israel and forgiveness of sins...
(Acts 5:31)

To him all the prophets bear witness that everyone who
believes in him receives forgiveness of sins through his name.
(Acts 10:43)

Let it be known to you therefore, brothers,
that through this man forgiveness of sins
is proclaimed to you...
(Acts 13:38)

Indeed, under the law almost everything
is purified with blood, and without the shedding of blood
there is no forgiveness of sins.
(Hebrews 9:22)

Author's Note

Because my Uncle Michael was such a special man and because of his encouragement and the large part he played in the first meeting with Daniel, I felt the need to reach out to his family and ask permission to use his real name in this book. I wanted to honour this gentle man of God, the late Reverend Arthur Michael Bensley.

In June of 2023, I received an email from my cousin, who said this about her father:

Dad leaned into asking God to grow and develop his character. His favourite verses are Galatians 5:22-23, which speak of the fruit of the spirit. Thank you so much, Miriam, for honouring your Uncle Michael in how you wrote about him. I can totally imagine him being your strength and prayerful support during one of the hardest times of your life, cheering you on with love and God's abundant blessings as you complete this very special book. It will bring hope and healing to many as they reach out to Jesus to help them with their own journey of life.

> *But when the Holy Spirit controls our lives, he will produce this kind of fruit in us: love, peace, patience, kindness, goodness, faithfulness, gentleness and self-control; and here there is no conflict with Jewish laws.*
> (Galatians 5:22-23 TLB)

*From Him, and through Him, and to Him, are all things.
To Him be the glory forever. Amen.*
(Romans 11:36)

Notes

Bible Copyrights

Scripture quotations marked NIV are taken from the Holy Bible, New International Version®, NIV®. Copyright © 1973, 1978, 1984, 2011 by Biblica, Inc.™ Used by permission of Zondervan. All rights reserved worldwide.

Scripture quotations marked CSB have been taken from the Christian Standard Bible®, Copyright © 2017 by Holman Bible Publishers. Used by permission. Christian Standard Bible® and CSB® are federally registered trademarks of Holman Bible Publishers.

Scripture quotations marked (TLB) are taken from The Living Bible, copyright © 1971 by Tyndale House Foundation. Used by permission of Tyndale House Publishers, Carol Stream, Illinois 60188. All rights reserved.

www.ingramcontent.com/pod-product-compliance
Lightning Source LLC
Chambersburg PA
CBHW011151290426
44109CB00025B/2565